D1175983

*Man and Beast
in American Comic Legend*

Man AND Beast

in American Comic Legend

RICHARD M. DORSON

Indiana University Press   BLOOMINGTON

Manufactured in the United States of America

Library of Congress Cataloging in Publication Data

Dorson, Richard Mercer, 1916–1981
   Man and beast in American comic legend.

   Includes bibliographical references.
   1. Legends—United States.   2. Tall tales—United States.   3. Animals, Mythical—United States.   I. Title.
GR105.D67 1982   398.2′0973   81-48622
ISBN 0–253–33665–1   AACR2
1 2 3 4 5 86 85 84 83 82

Contents

83-198

ACKNOWLEDGMENTS

Indiana University Press is grateful to Linda Johnson-Wells for bibliographical research and picture selection necessary for the completion of this posthumous publication.

The Press also wishes to thank those who have given permission to reproduce the following illustrations:

The Hodag: postcard by Antigo Card Service, Antigo, Wisconsin.

The Beast of 'Busco: From John A. Gutowski, "American Folklore and the Modern American Community Festival: A Case Study in Turtle Days in Churubusco, Indiana," Ph.D. diss., Indiana University, 1977. Photos courtesy *Fort Wayne News Sentinel.*

The Jackalope. Postcard by Petley Studios, Phoenix, Arizona. Bob Petley Photo.

Sasquatch tracks: Photos Rene Dahinden, Richmond, B.C., Canada. © Rene Dahinden 1967, 1969.

Johnny Darling: From M. Jagendorf, *The Marvelous Adventures of Johnny Darling* (New York: The Vanguard Press, 1949). Drawing by Howard Simon.

The Cherry-Tree Buck: From Frank L. Du Mond, *Tall Tales of the Catskills* (New York: Atheneum, 1968). Drawing by Peter Parnall.

Gib Morgan: From Mody C. Boatright, *Gib Morgan: Minstrel of the Oil Fields* (Austin: Texas Folk-Lore Society, 1945).

Jones Tracy: From C. Richard K. Lunt, *Jones Tracy: Tall-Tale Hero from Mount Desert Island* (Orono, Me.: The Northeast Folklore Society, 1969). Photograph loaned by Mr. and Mrs. Ralph Tracy.

Hathaway Jones: From Stephen Dow Beckham, *Tall Tales from Rogue River: The Yarns of Hathaway Jones* (Bloomington: Indiana University Press, 1974). Drawing by Christina Romano.

Introduction

It would normally be a total pleasure to welcome yet another fascinating excursion into American folklore guided by Richard M. Dorson, whose prolific pen has written or edited more than twenty-five earlier books on folklore. Yet in this case, the pleasure is offset by the sad thought that this is Professor Dorson's last book. Richard M. Dorson, Distinguished Professor of History and Folklore at Indiana University, and the dominant force in the academic study of folklore for the past twenty-five years, died on September 11, 1981. The present manuscript was one of several in the works—Professor Dorson was never content unless he was in the midst of a number of major research projects. Since two-thirds of the book as originally conceived was essentially in final form, and since the manuscript did present two valuable sets of sketches—of "fearsome critters" and "tall tale tellers"—Indiana University Press elected to publish *Man and Beast in American Comic Legend* as it was, even though it would obviously have been preferable if Professor Dorson could have written his own introduction and conclusion to the book. Instead, one of his children, Jeff, has added a sensitive remembrance of his father at work, and one of his many devoted students was invited to write a prefatory essay.

Born in New York City on March 12, 1916, Richard Mercer Dorson had the advantages of a fine education. After graduating from Phillips Exeter Academy in 1933, he began his Harvard years, receiving his A.B. in 1937, his M.A. in American History in 1940, and his Ph.D. in the History of American Civilization in 1943. Dorson was proud to be a Harvard alumnus and never tired of mentioning that fact whenever an opportunity presented itself. Following a year in which he served as an instructor in history at Harvard, he moved to Michigan State University, where he would remain for more than a dozen years (1944–1957). He used to tell an anecdote about his first year at Michigan State. Newly arrived on the campus, he was asked by the Department of History to give a course in Latin American history. Inasmuch as he was trained exclusively in North American history, he knew next to nothing about Latin America. Moreover, Spanish was not one of the foreign languages he controlled. Nevertheless, he had little choice, and so he dutifully prepared a series of lectures on Latin American history, hoping to keep just far enough ahead of the students to avoid any embarrassing questions. Evidently he succeeded, but as I recall, he taught the course only that one time.

During his Michigan State years, Richard Dorson's interests in folklore began to blossom. In 1946, he received a Library of Congress Fellowship in the History of American Civilization that enabled him to spend five months in the field in the tradition-rich Upper Peninsula of Michigan. This field experience changed Professor Dorson's life forever. Having once tasted the joys of gathering authentic oral materials from live informants (as opposed to reading literary, often bowdlerized, texts in print), Dorson spent the rest of his life in the field, whenever his busy teaching and administrative schedule would allow. The Upper Peninsula, then as now, offered a vast variety of folklore traditions. In his introduction to *Bloodstoppers and Bearwalkers* (Harvard University Press, 1952), a book that sampled these traditions, Dorson told of his excitement:

> The abundance and diversity of the oral traditions I found still stagger me. I heard creation myths, fairy tales, tall tales, occult tales, legends, romances, exploits, jests, anecdotes, noodle stories, dialect stories, told by Ojibwa, Potawatomi, and Sioux Indians; by Finns, Swedes, Poles, Germans, Italians, Irishmen, Frenchmen, Englishmen, even by Luxemburgers, Slovenians, and Lithuanians; by famers, lumberjacks, copper and iron miners, fishermen, sailors, railroaders, bartenders, undertakers, authors, county officials, newspaper editors; by the senile and the juvenile, the educated and the illiterate; by family circles and boarding house cliques in full blast and by solitary old-timers in tar paper shacks. I never spent a day in the Peninsula without collecting tales, even when several hours went in driving, and although I literally knew not a soul in the area.

The thrill of encountering American folklore in the flesh would never abate, and this genuine love of fieldwork would be enthusiastically communicated to his nearly one hundred doctoral degree students in folklore later at Indiana University.

Realizing that his fine Harvard education had not really prepared him for the finer points of carrying out fieldwork, Dorson decided to discover what anthropologists had to say on the subject. An American Council of Learned Societies Faculty Study Fellowship in 1952 permitted him to spend a post-doctoral year at Northwestern University with Professor Melville J. Herskovits, a first-generation student of Columbia's Franz Boas, who had pioneered the anthropological study of folklore in the United States. Herskovits had already become the leading scholar in African folklore, and his prize pupil, William R. Bascom, had stayed on at Northwestern. From Herskovits and Bascom, Dorson was introduced to cultural anthropology, and he soon learned that a proper folklorist needed both literary-historical training and anthropological field techniques. (Many of the older literary or library folklorists had never gone into the field to hear folklore firsthand, preferring instead to rely on the field reports of others.)

Perhaps partly inspired by Herskovits and Bascom, who were primarily concerned with African and Afro-American folktales, Dorson began to carry out fieldwork with black informants in Michigan. In 1952 and 1953, he recorded over a thousand oral narratives from Negroes living in the North but who were born in the South. *Negro Folktales in Michigan* was published by Harvard University Press in 1956. Later he visited the South—Pine Bluff, Arkansas, and Mound Bayou, Mississippi—to sample Afro-American traditions there. *Negro Tales from Pine Bluff, Arkansas, and Calvin, Michigan* was published in the Indiana University Folklore Series in 1958. It should be pointed out that Dorson was working with Afro-American folktales long before it became fashionable for white folklorists to do so. In contrast to Herskovits and Bascom, who claimed that Afro-American folktales came for the most part from Africa, Dorson believed the majority of the Afro-American narrative repertoire had a European origin. In *American Negro Folktales* (1967), a paperback anthology based on his earlier collections, Dorson stated his position in unequivocal terms: "The first declaration to make is that this body of tales does not come from Africa." Subsequent research has not tended to support Dorson's position—cf. Daniel Crowley, editor, *African Folklore in the New World* (1977); Florence Baer, *Sources and Analogues of the Uncle Remus Tales,* FFC 228 (Helsinki, 1980); and William Bascom's series of some twenty essays on individual African/Afro-American tale types appearing in *Research in African*

Literatures (1977ff.)—but the discipline of folkloristics remains in-
debted to Dorson for raising the issue in such scholarly terms.

By 1957, it was clear that Richard Dorson had become one of the
country's leading folklorists. When Stith Thompson, founder of Indiana University's doctoral degree program in folklore (the first
Ph.D. in folklore was awarded in 1953), retired, Dorson was one of
a small handful of individuals considered to replace him. Dorson
had risen to full professor at Michigan State; accordingly, in 1957,
when he moved to Indiana University, he was appointed Professor
of History and Folklore as well as Chairman of the Committee on
Folklore (that title was changed to Director of the Folklore Institute
in 1963).

At Indiana University, Richard Dorson's career continued to flour-
ish. *American Folklore* (published by the University of Chicago
Press in 1959) offered in a most readable format a chronological
overview of American folklore, from the colonial period to the twentieth century. From Dorson's experience as Fulbright Visiting Professor in American Studies at the University of Tokyo (1956–1957)
came two books: *Folk Legends of Japan* (1961) and *Studies in Japanese Folklore* (1963), an edited volume of translations. From 1957
to 1962 Dorson served as editor of the *Journal of American Folklore*.
In 1964, *Buying the Wind: Regional Folklore in the United States*
appeared; it provided a useful anthology of folklore materials for
some of the major regions in America. But it was in 1968 that perhaps Dorson's magnum opus was published, *The British Folklorists:
A History*. This volume reflected his deep love of England and things
English, his ever-present delight in history, and his passion for folklore. It is an authoritative survey of the beginnings of folklore scholarship in the English-speaking world, with fascinating sketches of
the individual folklorists in England who, especially at the end of
nineteenth century, helped form the discipline of folkloristics. *The
British Folklorists* was awarded the coveted Chicago Folklore
Prize—it was the third time Dorson had won it (his other prize-
winners were *Jonathan Draws the Long Bow,* 1947, and *Buying the
Wind,* 1965), a feat that would later be matched by his receiving his
third Guggenheim Fellowship (1949–1950, 1964–1965, 1971–1972).

Dorson's appointment at Indiana University in both history and
folklore was an appropriate one. Although he taught far more folklore than history courses, he did enjoy teaching American intellec-

tual history. Most of his teaching time was spent in such courses as seminars as American Folklore or Folklore Theory and Techniques. His dual allegiance to history and folklore found expression in *American Folklore and the Historian* (1971), a group of essays intended as much for the historian interested in folklore as for the folklorist interested in history. In his essay "A Theory for American Folklore," published in the *Journal of American Folklore* in 1959, Dorson argued that American folklore could not be studied without the background of American history. For Dorson, the two were inseparable. This viewpoint is reflected in the present volume, inasmuch as the beasts described were or are thought by some to be historical in nature—there are individuals who are convinced that Bigfoot exists; and the tall-tale tellers in the second part of this book are without exception historical individuals with known birth and death dates.

It is probably safe to say that Dorson's lasting contribution to folklore will lie in his delineation of the intersection of history and folklore. Of his two hundred-some essays, his classic historical account of "The Edipse of Solar Mythology," which appeared in the *Journal of American Folklore* in 1955, or "The Debate over the Trustworthiness of Oral Traditional History," which appeared in 1968 in Kurt Ranke's *festschrift* and was later reprinted in *Folklore: Selected Essays* (1972)—one of three published collections of Dorson's essays—are likely to be read and reread by future generations of folklore students. Of course, the field data he so lovingly elicited and reported will never go out of style. As Dorson moved intellectually from the library to the field, so he also moved from rural to urban fieldwork. His posthumously published *Land of the Millrats* (1981) presents a rich assortment of the folklore he found in the Calumet region of northwest Indiana, especially among steelworkers.

There is really no way to summarize adequately the writings of a workaholic who produced more than twenty-five books and two hundred articles in professional periodicals. And even if one were to attempt to review the thousands of pages of his writings, one would miss the tremendous energy Dorson devoted to attending and often organizing countless conferences on folklore. He traveled all over the world to champion the cause of folklore. From 1961 to 1981 he chaired the doctoral committees of nearly one hundred graduate students in folklore. It is a truly extraordinary record of achievement in both teaching and research. There can be no doubt that Richard Dorson thrived on the academic environment.

Yet no picture of Richard Dorson would be complete without some idea of his strong personality. He was extremely critical of what he considered shoddy or amateurish folklore scholarship, and he was not afraid to say so in person or in print. While one cannot help but admire the way in which he fought the good fight for folklore with funding agencies, fellowship committees, and publishing houses, it is also true that he was not above sending unsolicited letters of "nonrecommendation" when he felt a candidate or a proposal was not of high quality. In short, he made enemies—lots of them. The first time he was nominated for president of the American Folklore Society, in the early 1960s, there was an elaborate (and successful) attempt to defeat him. A last-minute nominee was proposed and elected at a frenzied business meeting at the New York City convention. Dorson had to wait two years to be elected president. His "enemies" hoped that this would humble him. It didn't! In a way, he was never happier than when he was engaged in some bitter dispute or feud with one folklorist or another. Much time and energy was devoted to attacking or counterattacking some hated rival or opponent of the moment. Frankly, most of the "enemies" were not worthy of him or his notice, but it was hard for his family or friends to reason with or restrain him. He was not an easy person to live with. He could not delegate responsibility, and he preferred to do everything himself, if at all possible. He wrote introductions to other scholars' books, e.g., in the multivolume Folktales of the World series, which he edited for the University of Chicago Press. Few scholars wrote introductions to *his* books, however, and he usually wrote his own prefaces or introductions.

Richard Dorson was unable to rest on his many laurels. He was always thinking about the research project about to be completed as well as the next one in the hopper plus one or two on the drawing board. He did take time out for tennis, which he thoroughly enjoyed all his adult life, and he was as competitive on the tennis court as he was in academic life. Sometimes it seemed that triumphs in tennis meant as much as the accolades of academe. In a letter to me dated June 15, 1971, he told me that Indiana University had rewarded his years of achievement by appointing him Distinguished

Professor of History and Folklore: "The Distinguished came through. It was on the same day that I scored an upset to enter the finals of the local tennis tournament. But the next day I was out on the court three hours in 90° heat and was only able to get within two points of victory." Not even repeated heart attacks during the last years of his life could keep him off the court. It was probably inevitable that his collapse on a tennis court in Bloomington, on June 28, 1981, occurred after a stirring singles match; he went into a coma from which he never recovered. It was only a question as to whether the final moment would come on the tennis court or in his study, immersed in galley proofs.

His family and friends had tried to get him to change his lifestyle in light of bypass heart surgery and various attacks thereafter, but to no avail. He continued to travel despite considerable discomfort. In a brief unpublished account of "A Folklore Trip to India," which he took in December 1978, we find this characteristic report of a night at the Airport Hotel in Calcutta:

> I lay immobile on a bed of pain, attacked from head to toe with chills and fever, nasal congestion, diarrhea, and gout, with a blood pressure of 170/100, due to fly in the morning to Gauhati. A jaunty doctor in white ducks appeared, chatted sociably while I deteriorated rapidly, prescribed some pills, asked for a memento from "so distinguished a scholar," whereupon I gave him an autographed copy of the *Journal of the Folklore Institute* [edited by Dorson], but unsatisfied he rummaged through my suitcase, held up my most luminescent ties, and asked for one. The pills worked, and I flew off the next morning, and will mail him a tie.

This adventure is immediately followed by a recollection of an afternoon on a mountainside in Assam.

> I watched outside Kamakhya Temple as priests ritually cut the heads off bleating goats, when a sudden sharp tug nearly pulled my own neck off, as a sacred cow devoured the garland my hosts had draped over my shoulders.

These anecdotes, which Dorson "did not report to the Smithsonian Institution, who kindly sponsored my Research Development Trip to plan for a Folktales of India volume in the Folktales of the World series," are quintessential Dorson: the lively, engaging writing style; the indomitable sense of humor, which he never lost, even in the face of increasingly serious medical problems; the highly developed ego mitigated somewhat by his own awareness of his egocentricity; and even his probably self-conscious selection of garish ties and socks.

In his last years, Dorson delighted in telling tales (memorates, actually—traditional personal semihistorical accounts) in which he figured as the central character. It is almost as though he identified with the historical characters about whom tall tales were told and who told many of these tales about themselves, that is, the characters whose exploits make up the second half of this volume. His personal feeling of identification with the American folklore he studied for so many years is revealed in a story Dorson told about himself. The incident occurred at Berkeley, California, during his stint as visiting professor in the spring of 1968. A nervy student in his lecture course on American folklore, sent him an anonymous note, asking, "When are you going to stop talking about yourself and start talking about American folklore?" Dorson told the class about the note and in telling the story to me and others, he added, "Don't they realize I *am* American folklore!" Well, in a way, he was absolutely right. Richard Dorson and American folklore are forever intertwined. It is inconceivable that anyone undertaking serious research in American folklore in the centuries to come will not have to consult his writings. If being read by scholars and students constitutes a kind of immortality, then Dorson's immortality is assured.

One can detect the seeds of *Man and Beast in American Comic Legend* in one of Professor Dorson's earliest works, *Jonathan Draws the Long Bow,* a survey of New England Legendary tales in print, published in 1946. Chapter IV of that book, entitled "Tall Tales," includes discussions of both "Munchausens" and the sea serpent, while the Windham Frog Fright is discussed in the opening chapter. In *Man and Beast,* we have a very typical example of Dorson scholarship. We find the interplay of folklore and history; we have the emphasis on comic legend that underscores Dorson's delight in humor; and we have the enormous respect for authentic oral texts coupled with the professional folklorist's disdain for altered or rewritten materials masquerading as the genuine article. We also have Dorson's disinclination to interpret the data he so assiduously gathered. He tended to be wary of symbolic and speculative analyses of folklore, fearing that too often they were read into rather than read out of the raw field data.

Yet the reader may well ask whether there is a significance to the legendary materials presented. Do accounts of strange beasts reveal something about Americans' attitudes toward nature or their own animality? Is the fact that the inhabitants of Windham were foolishly frightened by the sounds of frogs a parable suggesting that Americans must not be awed by nature, but must learn to conquer it? Animals that develop special physical features, allowing them to run around hills or to have two short legs to facilitate grazing on steep inclines might reflect our penchant for technological know-how, which allowed settlers to go around natural obstacles, such as inconveniently placed mountains, or to adapt in order to succeed in an unfriendly environment. Are the ongoing searches for sea serpents or Bigfoot (both with some obvious phallic connotations) a reflection of our romantic search for escape from the overly scientific world in which we live? The various scientific attempts to verify the existence of sea serpents or of Bigfoot creatures never quite succeed, and perhaps that is the point. The romance of the unknowable, or at any rate the not-yet-known, was part of the pull that led Americans westward, maybe even to the new frontiers of space travel. Even the blatant commerical motivations for the celebration of some of the fearsome critters Dorson surveys (e.g., the Jackalope, a combination of a jackrabbit and an antelope), suggest a pattern of creativity in which new creatures are conceived. In a New World in which old ethnicities and identities were often mixed, interbreeding was common. Many Americans are hyphenated-Americans, belonging to both the Old and New worlds. Some have mixed affiliations, with their fathers belonging to one ethnic group, their mothers to another. In this context, a Jackalope is an appropriate animal model or metaphor for such human interaction.

The two sections of *Man and Beast in American Comic Legend* share the theme of exaggeration. As animals possess fantastic features, so the tall-tale characters—it is no accident that the critical adjective is "tall"—perform fantastic feats. If the beasts represent the fantastic landscape challenging Americans, then the tall-tale heroes may signify the fantastic deeds of various pioneers. Whether it is a fabulous hunt or an ingenious technique of striking oil, big challenges require big characters to meet them. (Most of the tall-tale figures are male, suggesting something of a masculine bias in the American folklore in this volume. On the other hand, the folklore simply mirrors the bias of the society from which it comes.) But the American penchant for bragging and bigness may well mask an inferiority complex vis-à-vis Europe. America began as a series of colonies of European powers in which it was often the individuals who were unsuccessful in Europe who chose to move to the New World. To this day, many Americans continue to look to Europe for leadership in art, music, cuisine, fashion, diplomacy, etc.

In the same way that Americans feel inferior to Europeans, so many Americans in the West feel inferior to those living on the Atlantic seaboard. It may be no accident that the vast majority of tall tale tellers lived in the Midwest or West. The Eastern figures, John Darling and Jones Tracy, were definitely from isolated rural areas, the Catskill Mountains and Mount Desert Island. In any event, the American pleasure in boasting and the propensity to exaggerate may well be facets of national character related both to the historical facts of America's initial colonization and to the long-standing feelings of cultural inferiority. In this sense, one can almost detect a sense of pride in Americans' having their own mythical beasts, as opposed to the Europeans' dragons and unicorns.

Whatever the reasons why Americans have produced legendary creatures and enjoy tall tales, we can only be grateful to Richard Dorson for bringing together some of the data essential for speculating about such reasons. *Man and Beast in American Comic Legend* can be used profitably in conjunction with the extensive scholarship already in print on similar subjects. Unusual or fantastic animals have long fascinated folklorists. Angelo de Gubernatis, *Zoological Mythology,* 2 vols. (London: Trübner, 1872) and Eugène Rolland, *Faune populaire de la France,* 13 vols. (Paris: Maisonneuve, 1877–1911) both treat the folklore of animals. Most of the books tend to be popular surveys, e.g., John Ashton, *Curious Creatures in Zoology* (New York: Cassell, 1889), F. Edward Hulme, *Natural History: Lore and Legend* (London: Bernard Quaritch, 1895), Bernard Heuvelmans, *On the Track of Unknown Animals* (New York: Hill and Wang, 1959), and Jerome Clark and Loren Coleman, *Creatures of the Outer Edge* (New York: Warner Books, 1978). But there are occasional exceptions. For example, the proceedings of a conference on Sasquatch and Similar Phenomena held in May 1978, in British Columbia, were published in Marjorie M. Halpin and Michael M. Ames, editors, *Manlike Monsters on Trial: Early Records and Modern Evidence* (Vancouver: University of British Columbia Press, 1980). The book includes an extensive bibliography on,Bigfoot (pp. 316–334) as well as references to tall-tale traditions in Canada (p. 107, n.10). Other representative discussions of the tall tale include: Mody C. Boatright, "The Tall Tale in Texas," *South Atlantic Quarterly* 30 (1931):271–279; C. Grant Loomis, "The American Tall Tale and the Miraculous," *California Folklore Quarterly* 4 (1945):109–128; and Gustav Henningsen, "The Art of Perpendicular Lying," *Journal of the Folklore Institute* 2 (1965):180–219.

Readers who are not so concerned with the origin or social function or psychological significance of American fabulous beasts and tall tales may simply sit back and enjoy the volume. For the book is truly a marvelous one—full of marvels but also marvelous to read. And while we mourn the passing of an American scholar who was indeed a legend in his own time, we may yet celebrate one more achievement in *Man and Beast in American Comic Legend*. Exit laughing. That's the way Richard Dorson would have wanted it and that is how we shall remember him.

Alan Dundes

University of California, Berkeley

*Man and Beast
in American Comic Legend*

PART i

American Legendary Creatures

All the peoples of the world take seriously certain legendary creatures of a lower mythology with whom they associate on familiar terms. All, that is, save the people of the United States. Alexander H. Krappe once asserted that America possessed no folklore. What he should have said was that some of America's folklore differs from that of the rest of the world.

As examples of creatures of legend intimately bound with the culture, the lives, the psyche of a people, consider the fairies of Ireland, the kappa of Japan, and the jinn of Egypt. In common they possess supernatural powers; their existence is credited by a substantial sector of the national population; and their attributes are known to all in their land. The popular and the literary as well as the folk culture pay them tribute. They occupy only their own *patria*. (I once asked Sean O'Sullivan why the Irish in the United States do not sight fairies, and he opined that it was probably because the circles of greensward known as fairy rings on the Ould Sod did not appear in America.) These figures, in their various forms, live among their chosen folk, enter their homes, marry them on occasion, lurk in their gardens, fields, and streams, and transport them to other places. Yet the three also differ considerably from each other in their legendary lineaments.

The fairies take the shape of little green men and women, ani-

1

mals, ordinary human beings, and ghosts. Myriad are the memorates that recount meetings with the fairies by Irish farmer folk. In
the best of the collections about the fairy faith, *Visions and Beliefs
of the West of Ireland,* Lady Gregory set down cycles of testimonies
telling of neighbors who had been taken "away" by "them," or of
seeing harm come to those who traversed fairy routes, or of being
cured by healers in converse with the fairy people. In Dublin in
1951, lunching in the faculty dining room of University College
with folklorists Sean O'Sullivan and Kevin Danaher, I heard one of
their academic colleagues describe, with great intensity, how at the
age of two he had seen the fairies dancing on the green by a fairy
fort, which was desecrated shortly after by a workman, who died
within the year. Later in the week I visited the fieldworker in
County Kerry for the Irish Folklore Commission, Tadhg Murphy,
and heard him relate a lengthy experience that he had collected
from a narrator who had heard Sean Palmer tell how strangers had
taken him by boat in a few hours to America, where he called on
relatives. An elegant Yankee suit, a fine tobacco box, and a five-
dollar bill displayed by Sean Palmer next day convinced his wife
that he had indeed in one night visited America, thanks, of course,
to the fairies.[1]

Unlike the shape-shifting fairies, the kappa appears in one constant guise, that of a goblin-boy with a saucer-like cavity in its head.
If the fluid in the cavity is spilled, say by jostling the kappa, he loses
his malignant power. Kappas inhabit rivers, ponds and lakes, and
seize children swimming in the waters, or pull down horses and
cattle from the river banks, enter their anuses, draw out their intes-
tines, and suck their blood. Dictionaries and travel books describe
the kappa as an ugly naked child with greenish-yellow skin, a monkey face, a tortoise-like shell, webbed fingers and toes, and a fishy
smell. Kappas wrestle with men and rape women, but they have
their kinder side, too, and will teach the art of bonesetting to families that have befriended or captured them. In one tale a kappa fell
in love with the beautiful wife of a samurai and touched her but-
tocks as she sat on the toilet. Next night she took with her the short
sword of her husband and cut off the creature's hand as he stroked
her. The shaggy little man ran off shrieking, and night after night
appeared at the samurai's bed pleading for the return of his hand.
On receiving it he joined it to his arm, and the next day brought two

big fish to the samurai's garden and instructed him in setting broken bones.[2]

The kappa permeates Japanese culture. He appears as a character in novels, short stories, comic cartoons; his likeness is depicted in wood carvings, on place mats, checks, and on television. In the summer of 1975 in a Tokyo hotel, I saw on my color TV a documentary on the kappa, with scenes of farmers pointing out to the interviewer streams where the goblin resided. Although the camera did not catch a live kappa, inserted stills of kappa drawings indicated plainly enough the subject of the animated discussion.

Even more than the fairies and the kappas, the jinn live close to the homes of men. In Cairo they occupy old houses, ovens, latrines, baths, and wells; they take the form of cats, dogs, men, and monsters, or become invisible. Created before Adam, they resemble the human species, but live for centuries and perpetrate magical mischief. Malicious jinn perched on rooftops hurl bricks and stones into the streets and courts of Cairo and other cities in Egypt. Some human magicians of unusual powers are believed to have obtained them from marrying a female jinni. During the first ten days of Moharram, a jinni in the form of a water-carrier knocks at the door of a sleeping person, who calls out, "Who is there?" The jinni responds, "I, the water-carrier; where shall I empty the skin?" "Empty into the water-jar," ritually states the lucky one, aware that water-carriers do not come at night, and later he finds the jar full of gold. Sometimes the jinni arrives in the form of a mule bearing saddlebags full of gold and a dead man's head upon his back.[3] Evil jinn known as ghouls haunt burial grounds and feed on dead bodies and the living who happen to come their way. Egyptians of the Islamic faith utter various charms against the jinn, such as "Iron, thou unlucky!" especially when they see approaching across the desert a whirlwind of sand caused by the flight of a jinni.

Examples could readily be multiplied of these supernatural-legendary-mythological beings who mingle intimately with the peoples to whose culture they belong and enter their personal experience tales. This past year, Martha Blache of Argentina completed a doctoral dissertation in folklore at Indiana University on memorates and anecdotes of such beings that she collected from the Guarani Indians.[4] She speaks of the *pombero,* a small fairy whose friendship and protection may be cultivated with offerings left outside the house; of the *yasy yateré,* a pretty, fairhaired creature that whistles and entices children into the woods at noon; and the *luisón,* the seventh son of an uninterrupted series of boys, a thin, ailing, unsociable man by day, and a dog that feeds on dead bodies on Friday nights.

The mainstream culture of the United States exhibits no directly comparable creatures. We were born too late to develop a higher or lower mythology, and unlike our northern and southern neighbors, we excluded the Native American, erased the Afro-American, and suppressed the ethnic American goblins from our folk-belief system. The winds of rationalism and secularism blew away these uprooted traditions, even the ubiquitous Devil once regularly sighted in the seventeenth century.

Instead we have acquired a comic mythology of "fearsome critters" who perform services and reflect the United States ethos in a manner comparable to the roles of the kappas, jinn, and fairy folk. We yarn about, identify with, hunt for, depict, extol, and chuckle over these critters. Belief and dread are not wholly absent, but in contrast to the rest of the world, we engage in hoaxes, pranks, tall tales, and tomfoolery with our legendary creatures. I have nominated ten zoological marvels for the American Hall of Fearsome Critters, selecting them on the basis of longevity, in terms of our short history; recognition by tale tellers, boosters, and bards; a modicum of credence; and a large dash of extravaganza, American style.

Various ingredients have contributed to this domesticated animal kingdom—the medieval bestiary, the Munchausen vein of fanciful quadrupeds, explorers' and travelers' tales of New World monsters— but these American specimens have reached a special plateau. They are no longer creatures out there, in the forests, the rivers, and the mountains, but creatures within our culture, in our towns, our county fairs, our family circles.

First, a word on sources. The folklorist investigating America's imaginary animals finds a paucity of field-collected texts—a general difficulty with all American folk narrative, as I once heard Ernest Baughman remark. Particularly with these fearsome critters is the problem of locating oral texts accentuated, since they rarely do anything; the narrative action is lacking; what counts is the mere existence of these grotesque species, verified in terms of their appearance and habits. So descriptions of the beasts easily take the form of loose paraphrase or generalized accounts. Only in the case of the hoopsnake, who does perform an action—rolling like a hoop, chasing a man, and striking his stinger into a tree, which shortly withers and dies—and the sidehill dodger, who can be caught by being turned around, are manifold texts available. The Windham frogs did participate in an event but long before the days of field collecting, so for their escapade we rely on literary texts. Furthermore, the total complex of the critter's tradition involves more than a tale, since community response, tourist interest, hoax perpetration, protofestival activities, and media and literary recognition come into play and require ethnographic treatment and analysis. Excellent studies of these phenomena are John Gutowski's dissertation on Oscar the Turtle and William Harris's article on the White River Monster, which will be cited in due course.

The best single source, although not a collection of oral texts, is a comic bestiary titled *Fearsome Creatures of the Lumberwoods, with a Few Desert and Mountain Beasts,* which appeared in 1910, before the emergence of the Paul Bunyan pseudo-legend. William T. Cox wrote a one-page description of each of the twenty bizarre animals. Coert DuBois illustrated each on a facing page with poker-faced drawings, and the press of Judd and Detweiler in Washington, D.C., issued the forty-seven page book. Cox, who died in 1961 at the age of 82, graduated from the first class in forestry at the University of Minnesota, served as Minnesota's first State Forester (1911) and first Conservation Commissioner (1931) and conducted a widely read column in *The Farmer,* as well as writing little books on *Bird Stories* and *Wild Animals of Field and Forest.*[5] In his introduction to *Fearsome Creatures,* Cox maintained that lumberjacks had devised these mythical monsters as part of their imaginary oral lore. He wrote:

> Thrilling tales of adventure are told in camp wherever the logger has entered the wilderness. The lumberjack is an imaginative being, and a story loses none of its interest as it is carried and repeated from one camp to another. Stories which I know to have originated on the Penobscot and the Kennebec are told, somewhat strengthened and improved, in the redwood camps of Humboldt Bay. Yarns originating among the river drivers of the Ottawa, the St. Croix, and the upper Mississippi are re-spun to groups of listening loggers on Vancouver Island. But every lumber district has its own peculiar tales. Some have their songs

The Snoligoster

also, and nearly all have mysterious stories or vague rumors of
dreadful beasts with which to regale newcomers and frighten
people unfamiliar with the woods.[6]

In his little book Cox put on record some of these frightening
creatures dreamed up by the lumberjacks. Whether he, or they, or
both did most of the imagining, some curious fauna resulted. Cox
classified each of the Twenty with mock-Latin taxonomic labels and
solemnly presented details of their physiology and predatory traits.
The roperite, found in the Sierra foothills and said by the Digger
Indians to be the spirits of early Spanish ranchers, half flies, half
bounds across rugged terrain to pursue and snare its prey, meanwhile whirring the rattles on its tail. The snoligoster resembles a
crocodile but lacks legs or fins save for one long spike on its back on
which it impales outlaws in the swamps of Lake Okeechobee in
Florida; three bony plates revolving on its tail drive it through the
mud at the speed of a torpedo boat. The slide-rock bolter lurks on
steep Colorado mountain slopes watching for summer tourists, and
on sighting one or more lifts its tail (constructed with grab-hooks to
catch a mountain crest) and slides down the mountain like a tobog-

gan, drooling skid grease from the corners of its mouth to accelerate its speed, until it gulps down its prey. A forest ranger once plotted the destruction of a slide-rock bolter, as follows:

> A dummy tourist was rigged up with plaid Norfolk jacket, knee breeches, and a guide book to Colorado. It was then filled full of giant powder and fulminate caps and posted in a conspicuous place, where, sure enough, the next day it attracted the attention of a bolter which had been hanging for days on the slope of Lizzard Head. The resulting explosion flattened half the buildings in Rico, which were never rebuilt, and the surrounding hills fattened flocks of buzzards the rest of the summer.[7]

In 1939 Henry H. Tryon produced a volume closely imitating Cox's original comic bestiary, even to the title *Fearsome Critters*. The author claimed that he had collected logging tales in the camps and on the drives of "legendary woods varmints" for the past thirty years, and dated his first hearing of one, the tree-squeak, in 1908, even to remembering how two woods narrators gulled a greenhorn with details about the creature in a back-and-forth sober exchange. Tryon speculates that such tales may have existed for a century or more, although woodsmen who began working in the 1870s and '80s told him they did not hear them until the turn of the century. He declares that the Hodag, the tree-squeak, and the Side-Hill Gouger had been well known in the Northeast seventy years earlier and had migrated westward with the logging industry. Many correspondents submitted critters to him, several of which he excluded from his book because of their limited range but mentioned in his preface.

Tryon acknowledges his debt to William T. Cox, as indeed he should since he adapts eleven of Cox's twenty beasts into his own bestiary of thirty-one alphabetically arranged critters. He also thanks Charles E. Brown (whose name he misspells Browne) and Lake Shore Kearney (whose book he misspells *Hugah*). Still he appears to have tapped some oral information and mentions a "veteran guide" of the White Mountains and a professor of forestry in New York as informants. The format follows Cox, with full-page illustrations facing the text describing the animal, and the comic Latin identifications underneath the animal's name, but all is inferior; the wooden drawings, by Margaret Ramsay Tryon, match the prose style.[8]

The Tripodero

In a paragraph in his book on *Hoaxes* in 1940, Curtis MacDougall mentions some mythical timberlands creatures. Those also described by Cox include the whirling whimpus, which according to MacDougall "spins like a top so rapidly that its physical characteristics cannot be determined." According to Cox, who locates the beast in the Cumberland Mountains of Tennessee, it resembles a gorilla save for tiny hind legs, on which it stands at a bend in the trail and whirls until it becomes invisible, whereupon any chance passer-by, human or animal, who crosses its path will be "deposited in the form of syrup or varnish upon the huge paws of the whimpus."[9] MacDougall also cites the tripodero and agrees with Cox that it has telescopic legs like a photographer's tripod, which it extends to see above the chaparral in the California foothills and, sighting game with its large snout, fires clay quids from its left jaw demolishing its victim. The tripodero then contracts its legs and bores through the brush to its prey.[10] Not mentioned by Cox are the rubberado and the rackabore (see below), as well as a series of critters that MacDougall merely enumerates: the wampus cat, tree-squeak, cross-feathered snee, snow snake, and snoligostus. This last presumably is a variant of Cox's snoligoster but is not described.

Likenesses of two of Cox's bestiary appear on a page of illustrations in *Hoaxes* captioned "Improbable quadrupeds: the Whirling Whimpus spinning like a top and the Tripodero on four elongated legs with a tiny tail." They vary considerably from Cox's drawings. Cox's tripodero has but two legs and a thick tail reaching the ground, to give a true tripod effect, while his whirling whimpus depicts a gorilla-like creature on dainty legs lurking behind a tree awaiting a wanderer coming along the path. In addition MacDougall's page presents a variant of the sidehill dodger: "The Rackabore, an offspring of the javelina, is legged for sidehills. There are two types, right and left-handed." Completing the quartet of quadrupeds is the rubberado, a balloon-like animal shown in midair, which "bounces when shot. Anyone who eats it, bounces too." Possibly the rubberado is a distant kin to Cox's bearlike gumberoo, off whose elastic hide any bullet or missile bounces back at the attacker.[11] MacDougall lists his source simply as "Outdoor Life" and provides the accompanying statement: "Tenderfeet on camping trips are thrilled by the stories old-timers tell them of fabulous beasts. If they existed, some of these creatures would look like this."[12]

A third comic bestiary of 1976 following the format of Cox and Tryon, but adapted for a younger audience, carries the title *Kickle Snifters and Other Fearsome Critters, Collected from American Folklore,* by Alvin Schwartz, author of several comparable works of juvenile folklore, all illustrated with comical line drawings by Glen Rounds, who earlier illustrated his own Paul Bunyan book. This edition presents simplified texts in large type with the overcute drawings frequently on the same pages as the text. Schwartz commendably provides a statement on "Notes and Sources" indicating the provenience of his twenty-seven creatures, and a useful "Bibliography" of twenty entries.[13] He candidly acknowledges: "Except for a passage from 'The Raggedy Man' [by James Whitcomb Riley] all references have been adapted and many have been embellished."[14]

From Cox to Tryon to Schwartz the ferocity of the fearsome critters is noticeably softened, and we may assume thereby the closer relation to oral tradition in Cox, who is not only the first but also the toughest. Thus the alligator-like snoligoster in Cox reappears

neither in Tryon nor in Schwartz nor anywhere else in the printed
sources, for reasons clear to a reader of the following paragraph:

> Mr. Inman F. Eldredge, of De Funiak Springs, Florida, while
> hunting for an outlaw negro in the swamps, had a most unusual
> experience. He caught sight of the negro, dead and impaled upon
> what at first appeared to be a slender cypress knee, but which
> presently began to move away. It was then seen to be the spike
> on a snoligoster's back. Eldredge's first impulse was to shoot the
> strange beast, but upon second thought he concluded that it was
> doing a good work and was entitled to live on. The very report of
> such a creature inhabiting the swamps would deter evil-doers
> from venturing into these wild places to avoid their pursuers
> and escape justice.[15]

The facing illustration shows the hapless runaway lying face up-
wards on the snoligoster's back with the spike protruding through
his midriff. Hardly stuff for kids, or for many adults. While
Schwartz does borrow the slide-rock bolter from Cox, the later
writer substitutes spiders for the parties of tourists that Cox's bolter
enjoys gulping down.

To the three comparable bestiaries of Cox, Tryon, and Schwartz
we may join the unillustrated eight-page booklet of Charles E.
Brown, *Paul Bunyan Natural History* (1935), recording seventeen
animals, six fish, five birds, and two bugs noted for remarkable
properties.[16] Matching Brown's critters with Cox's twenty, Tryon's
thirty-one, and Schwartz's twenty-seven, we find these duplications.
One beast alone, the tripodero, enters all four bestiaries. Thirteen
enter three: the hugag, splinter cat, and squonk turn up in all except
Brown; the hidebehind, hoopsnake, and sidehill dodger appear in
all except Cox; the agropelter, gumberoo, hodag, and roperite occur
in all except Schwartz.

Mention should be made of Charles M. Skinner's *American Myths
and Legends,* appearing in 1903, seven years earlier than Cox,
which provides separate evidence for American oral tradition of
mythical animals. Skinner indulged in somber and romantic legends, lacking any sources and written up with literary gloss, but in
many cases demonstrably based on the stuff of tradition, and in his
section on "Maine's Woodland Terrors" he has placed on early record
four strange creatures, described to greenhorns in camps by seasoned lumberjacks. Best known is the sidehill dodger, whose down-

The Squonk

hill legs grow longer than his uphill ones; this rabbit-like specimen is so-called because "he winds about steep hills in only one direction."[17] Less familiar is the will-am-alone, of the squirrel family, which rolls poisonous lichens into pellets and drops them into the ears and onto the eyelids of sleeping lumberjacks, particularly the hardest drinkers, causing them headaches and nightmares and visions of strange objects in the snow. Eating the fat of a winder, if one can be caught, cures the illness caused by the will-am-alone. The ding-ball, cousin to the panther, cracks the skulls of human victims with its ball-shaped tail, and lures them into the darkness with sweet songs. Most dreaded is the windigo, who shares with the Bigfoot genus the size of his footprint, twenty-four inches long, and his humanoid appearance, "dark and huge and shadowy."[18] In the middle of each print a red spot shows where blood has oozed through his moccasin. To look upon the windigo is death, in the Indian belief, a belief so deeply held that an Irishman in a Canadian lumber district scared away a number of Indian woodchoppers by tramping through their camp in fur-covered snowshoes and squeezing into each print a drop of red paint, or perhaps beef blood.

The Hugag

The comic bestiaries and scattered articles about imaginary animals provide but one type of source for the fearsome critters I have nominated for American zoomythological stardom. All ten creatures selected meet the following criteria:

1. They enjoy a life in oral anecdote and tradition. Although the field-recorded texts desired by the folklorist are all too frequently wanting, strong evidence exists through paraphrase, reference, and literary versions of collectable verbal forms. Veteran woodsmen gulled tenderfeet with tales of imaginary animals; sober citizens repeated accounts of monsters sighted; laughing narrators related episodes of practical jokes and hoaxes involving the "fearsome critters." For lack of sufficient oral vigor Paul Bunyan and Babe the Blue Ox, for example, fail to qualify.

2. They inspire belief and conviction as well as hilarity and tomfoolery. Greenhorns accept the existence of the sidehill dodger, the hodag, the hugag, and their kin. The residents of Windham in 1784 did mistake thirsty frogs for marauding Indians. Colonial settlers credited the powers of the hoopsnake and the sea serpent. Some

The Hodag

scientists today devoutly believe in the reality of Bigfoot. The first discoverer of Oscar the Turtle of Churubusco devoted all his energies to tracking down the great turtle and confounding his skeptics. Those who fled from the guyuscutus acknowledged his existence by their flight, and visitors to county fairs gawked at the hodag.

3. They have in most cases endured for a considerable period of American history. From the colonial era come the sea serpent (known before the discovery of America), the Hoopsnake, the Windham Frogs. Julius Caesar described the animal that couldn't lie down. Ante-bellum sketches inform us about the Guyuscutus and the Sidehill Beast. Eugene Shepard launched the Hodag at the turn of the present century. Bigfoot has been sighted since the 1920s. Only Oscar the Turtle and the Jackalope are youngsters.

4. They have become personalized and institutionalized. Our ten critters possess charisma and folk—or pseudo-folk—appeal. Other contending beasts in Cox's bestiary have exerted no comparable impact on the American imagination. Chambers of Commerce have adopted Bigfoot, Oscar the Turtle, the Jackalope, the Hodag. The Free Public Library of Windham memorializes the Bullfrogs. Mark Twain adapted the Guyuscutus. Tale tellers all over the country yarn about the Sidehill Beast and the Hoopsnake. Newspaper sto-

ries feature sea serpents and lake monsters. By contrast the rattle-snake, for instance, which shares with the Hoopsnake tall tales about its sting causing wood or iron to swell, has not acquired folk popularity nor an individual personality, for the rattlesnake indu-bitably exists.

5. They are all fanciful—mythical if you will. No one has yet captured an authentic specimen of any of the fearsome critters. An exception may be made for the Windham Frogs, but their blowup into an invading army took on a fictional quality. Yet all possess their own reality, for all have been seen or heard and talked about, and have become household familiars.

6. They all have their comical side, presented in spoof, gag, prank, and whopper, which endear them to American publics. No such hu-morous endearment yet characterizes the UFOs, who remain out there in space, figures of not all that close encounters, treated still too reverently to tickle the American palate.

Only two of my ten appear in Cox, and one of these deviates wholly from the tradition elsewhere recorded. The roperite, only critter to make all four bestiaries, does not make my ten. Four of my ten do score triples in the bestiary match-ups.

Collectively they support my theory for American (i.e., United States) folklore, that the special conditions of American history have shaped the character of American folklore. In place of a lower mythology we have recourse to a comic bestiary.

ONE

The Windham Frogs

IN the words of a local antiquarian, Lillian Marsh Higbee, an army of thirsty frogs who terrorized the inhabitants of Windham, Connecticut, one June night in 1754, "rendered this old-fashioned town famous for all time."[19] The frogs put Windham on the map. At the time of the episode a thousand souls resided in the frontier village, and all lived in apprehension of French and Indian attack. Colonel Eliphalet Dyer had just raised a regiment to join the British expedition against Crown Point in New York, and other citizens had taken the field with General Israel Putnam to battle the "savages." In this atmosphere occurred the event customarily alluded to as the Frog Fight, or the Frog Fright, which was first recounted *in extenso* in 1781 by the Reverend Samuel Peters in his folklore-filled *General History of Connecticut,* as follows:

> Strangers are very much terrified at the hideous noise made on summer evenings by the vast number of frogs in the brooks and ponds. There are about thirty different voices among them, some of which resemble the bellowing of a bull. The owls and whippoorwills complete the rough concert, which may be heard several miles. Persons accustomed to such serenades are not disturbed by them at their proper stations; but one night in July, 1758 [*sic*], the frogs of an artificial pond, three miles square, and about five from Windham, finding the water dried up, left the

15

place in a body, and marched, or rather hopped, towards Winno-
mantic River. They were under the necessity of taking the road
and going through the town, which they entered about midnight.
The bull-frogs were the leaders, and the pipers followed without
number. They filled the road, forty yards wide, for four miles in
length, and were for several hours in passing through the town
unusually clamorous.

The inhabitants were equally perplexed and frightened: some
expected to find an army of French and Indians; others feared an
earthquake, and dissolution of Nature. The consternation was
universal. Old and young, male and female, fled naked from
their beds, with worse shriekings than those of the frogs. The
event was fatal to several women. The men, after a flight of half
a mile, in which they met with many broken shins, finding no
enemies in pursuit of them, made a halt, and summoned resolution enough to venture back to their wives and children, when
they distinctly heard from the enemy's camp these words: Wight,
Hilderkin, Dier, Tete. This last, they thought, meant treaty, and,
plucking up courage, they sent a triumvirate to capitulate with
the supposed French and Indians. These the men approached in
their shirts, and begged to speak with the general; but, it being
dark and no answer given, they were sorely agitated for some
time betwixt hope and fear: at length, however, they discovered
that the dreaded inimical army was an army of thirsty frogs
going to the river for a little water.

Such an incursion was never known before nor since; and yet
the people of Windham have been ridiculed for their timidity on
this occasion. I verily believe an army under the Duke of Marl-
borough would, under like circumstances, have acted no better
than they did.[20]

Higbee (writing in 1930) notes that Peters set the date four years
after the event, missed the site of the battle by four miles, and
inflated the number of frogs into the millions,[21] but no one can
accuse Peters of fabricating the tale. Too many eye-witnesses
talked, and the tale grew rapidly into legend. Within a month Ezra
Stiles, Yale's learned president, was writing a letter to his nephew
from Woodstock, on July 9, 1754, spoofing "the late tragical tidings
from Windham" with jives at lawyers and remorseless puns upon
the name of Colonel Dyer: "Dyerful ye alarm made by these audacious, long winded croakers. Things unattempted yet in prose
or rhyme, Tauranean terrors in Chimeras Dyer. I hope sir, from
the Dyerful reports from the frog pond, you'll gain some instruc-
tion. . . ."[22] When Windham County historian Ellen D. Larned pub-

lished her chronicle in 1874, she inserted a version of the Frog
Fright transmitted orally for 120 years, told by the wife of Colonel
Dyer's Negro servant to a lad, George Webb, who remembered this
account in old age:

> Well, it was in June I think, and the weather was very hot,
> and master had drawn off the pond to fix the dam. When he came
> home he did not think of nothing. By and by when it became cool,
> there began to be a rumble, rumble, rumble in the air, and it
> grew louder and louder and louder, and seemed to be like drums
> beating in the air. Well, it was in the old French war, when our
> men had gone to Belle Isle or Canada to fight the French and
> Indians, and some guessed it was the Ingins having a pow-wow
> or war dance on Chewink Plain, and we should all be killed in
> the morning.
>
> But Master (Col. Dyer), and Col. Elderkin and Mr. Gray
> mounted their horses and rode to the top of Mullin Hill, as the
> pond was a little way over there beyond. Master said he supposed
> the frogs fought each other, for the next day there were thou-
> sands of them dead. They croaked some the next night, but noth-
> ing so bad.[23]

Thus the plain unvarnished tale, which contended against many
improved and poetical renderings. In one of these effusions, "A True
Relation of a Strange Battle Between Some Lawyers and Bull-Frogs
Set Forth in a New Song, Written by a Jolly Farmer of New England," composed by Ebenezer Tilden of Lebanon, one verse does
allude to the servant-informant:

> A negro man, we understand,
>   Awoke and heard the shouting,
> He ne'er went abroad, but awaked his lord
>   Which filled their hearts with doubting.

The moral of the ballad, already set forth in Stiles's letter, proves
to be the just humiliation of the lawyers of Windham:

> Lawyers, I say, now from this day,
>   Be honest in your dealing,
> And nevermore increase your store,
>   While you the poor are killing.[24]

The picture of sedate town elders and pettifogging lawyers in
their nightdress being routed by thirsty frogs delighted colonial

Americans, who must have repeated the incident endlessly. According to the county historian:

> The story flew all over the County with innumerable additions
> and exaggerations. . . . Nor was the report of the Windham panic
> confined to its own County. Even without the aid of newspapers
> and pictorial illustrations, it was borne to every part of the land.
> It was sung in song and ballad; it was related in histories; it
> served as a standing joke in all circles and seasons. Few inci-
> dents occurring in America have been so widely circulated.[25]

Evidence for the oral popularity of the episode can be seen in the numerous recountings in prose and verse that appeared in the humor-hungry ante-bellum press. In the course of my own researches in the periodicals of the 1850s, looking for Yankee yarns, I happened upon the following: Ebenezer Tilden's "The Bull Frog Fight, A Ballad of the Olden Time," printed in forty-four verses in the *Boston Museum* in 1851; "The Frogs of Windham," in the Burlington, Vermont, *Daily Free Press,* May 12, 1853; "Something More About Frogs," in the Boston *Portfolio,* December 20, 1856; "The Windham Bank-Bills, and Connecticut Frogs," in the New York *Spirit of the Times* 26 (January 24, 1857):591. Local histories and legend books invariably presented a version with their own novel touches. In 1882, "Shepherd Tom" Hazard, musing on bullfrogs in his Rhode Island bag of traditions, recollected the affair and stressed the thrilling cry of "Colonel Dyre, Colonel Dyre" exclaimed by the traveling bullfrogs. He concluded: "The men of Windham, it was said, ever after this had a special antipathy to bull-frogs, and made a point of conscience and honor to destroy every one they could find trespassing on their domain."[26] Charles M. Skinner, in his popular legend tomes of 1897, *Myths and Legends of Our Own Land,* duly wrote on "The Windham Frogs" and added a note on the two lawyers, Colonel Dyer and Mr. Elderkin, who were running against each other for office. Townspeople swore they heard yells of "Colonel Dyer" followed by a guttural response, "Elderkin, too!" On discovering the frogs next day, they interpreted the piping of the smaller ones as sounding like "Colonel Dyer" and the grumble of the bullfrogs as "Elderkin, too."[27]

In the nineteenth and twentieth centuries the Windhamites turned the tradition to their own advantage by promoting rather than suppressing the affair. The bank the Windham issued bank-notes in the 1850s bearing the likeness of two frogs, and samples are on display today in the Windham Library. For the 1892 bicentennial celebration of the founding of Windham, Theron Brown, an editor of *Youth's Companion,* composed and read a twelve-page poem, "The Epic of Windham," later published in the souvenir booklet of the occasion.[28] The "Epic" paid particular attention to the bullfrogs, even to reciting a list of fifty-four personal names, and including bits of dialogue expressing their disgruntlement when the miller drew water from the pond while he tinkered with the dam:

> "Cudderow, cudderow," grumbled little and great,
> "You Plug," said old Popeye, "You plague," said his mate.
> "Jug-o-rum," thundered Yellowthroat, "Slum," echoed back
> The meaniest and wartiest sneak in the pack.[29]

The town fathers honored Frog Pond with a bronze tablet set in a large granite boulder, which they dedicated on Constitution Day, September 24, 1924. Its inscription reads:

THIS TABLET IS ERECTED BY
ANNE WOOD ELDERKIN CHAPTER D.A.R.
TO COMMEMORATE THE LEGEND OF THE BATTLE OF THE FROGS

But when architects in planning the new Town Hall showed designs for two granite slabs in front of the hall exhibiting two giant granite frogs, the town fathers withheld approval.

Higbee's twenty-six page booklet, *Bacchus of Windham and the Frog Fright,* is currently distributed by the Windham Free Library. Her first topic dealt with "a quaint, curious, authentic Revolutionary relic," to wit a Cupid-like image of Bacchus straddling a keg marked 1776 and holding a basket of grapes. Four English prisoners of war held in the Windham jail during the Revolution used jack-knives to carve the image and keg, 26½ inches high and 21 inches long, probably in imitation of a ship's figurehead, and gave it to the wife of a local tavern keeper who assisted their escape. The widow Carey subsequently used it as a tavern sign. Alongside her account of this treasured memorial of Windham history, deeded to the Windham Free Library Association, Higbee narrated "A Mystery of 1754, An Account of the Batrachian Battle, the Tale of Deflated Greenbacks," pieced from the verse and prose accounts of the matter, and documented with photographs of the Windham Frog Pond and the memorial tablet. Higbee's booklet represents the appeal of traditional folk history as opposed to conventional textbook history.

The Windham Free Library additionally memorializes the aborted battle of 1754 with a bookplate bearing its name above a figure of a hefty frog standing on its hind legs, with its forepaws outstretched, in a human posture. In a letter to me dated June 4, 1974, the then librarian, Amy L. Anderson, wrote that "The 'Frog' is used as an emblem in the Town of Windham." Further substantiating this point she enclosed four attractive postcards illustrated with drawings, reproduced in a soft green shade, that concern the Frog Fright. One, labeled "Southwestern view of the Frog Pond in 1838," presents a pastoral scene of a New England countryside with a back road, stone fence, and small farmhouse in the foreground, a meadow and the pond and a row of pine trees in the background. No sign of a frog, but in three other postcards they dominate the scenes. In "Windham Frogs before the Battle in 1754" two mammoth bullfrogs confront each other on dry land. In "Windham Frogs after the Battle in 1754," three apprehensive looking males in nightdress, one carrying a flag of truce, eye the flattened bodies of frogs in the distance while before them one jolly frog prances on one foot atop a fencepost. In "Frogs of Windham," the top caption, coupled with a smaller bottom caption, "Voices of the Night," four man-sized frogs sit on a fallen branch across a pond, their feet dangling in the water and holding what seem like hymnbooks, while another on the bank plays a fiddle and a smaller chap facing them leads the chorus with his hands.

As the county historian wrote in 1874, "Let a son of Windham penetrate to the uttermost parts of the Earth, he would find that the story of the Frog-fright had preceded him. The Windham Bull-Frogs have achieved a world-wide reputation, and with Rome's goose, Putnam's wolf and a few other favored animals, will ever hold a place in popular memory and favor."[30]

Apart from their escapade in Windham, frogs have made an impact on American folklore from several fronts: their emulation of human speech, their girth, and their jumping abilities. Ernest Baughman assigns a motif to "Frogs cries misunderstood" (J1811.5*), and cities, in addition to the frogs of Windham, episodes from Massachusetts, New Jersey, North Carolina, Mississippi, Indi-

ana, and Texas in which simpletons respond to imagined utterances
of frogs. The words vary widely, from "Ketch Eddy! Eat him up!" to
"Knee deep! Chicken waded!" to "Old Hads! Drunk again! Let's pull
him in! Drown him!"[31]

The size and sounds of bullfrogs attracted the attention of colonial
naturalists and travelers. In 1663 the Jesuit father Hierosme Lale-
ment referred to frogs in the Huron territory "as large as dinner-
plates, whose voice is similar to the bellowing of bulls." In 1791
William Bartram recorded the size of bullfrogs in Virginia as attain-
ing eighteen inches and noted that they roared like bulls.[32] But it
was in Louisiana that the character of bullfrogs became the subject
of a spirited debate, one which formed part of a much larger contro-
versy, the character of America itself. The anti-Americanists, led by
the Dutch philosopher Corneille De Paw, disparaged everything
American as degenerate and diseased. The pro-Americanists, cham-
pioned by Antoine Josephe de Pernety, a chaplain of Bougainville,
extolled and exalted everything American. The exaggeration-prone
Father Louis Hennepin in his *Description de la Lousiane* in 1688
speaks of "frogs of an unusual size, whose croaking is as strong as
the bellowing of bulls." The term bullfrog originates with that observation. But it was the statement attributed to Dumont de Mon-
tigny in 1753 in his *Mémoires historiques sur la Louisiane* which
both DePaw and Pernety fastened upon to advance their arguments.
This statement, of dubious authorship as well as veracity, described
a gigantic species of frogs large as a seal weighing up to thirty-
seven pounds, with eyes like those of a bull, who bellowed like cows.
According to their respective interpretations, De Paw seized on
these "facts" as evidence of American monstrosity, and Pernety of
American fecundity.[33]

Yet from Texas in the twentieth century come assertions to support the seemingly exaggerated claims of the sound and stretch of
bullfrogs in eighteenth-century Louisiana. The naturalist Roy Be-
dichek reports instances of frogs swallowing a duckling's head, hum-
mingbirds on the wing, and an eleven-inch alligator.[34]

Folkloric frogs could be expected to jump prodigiously, and they
did, most notoriously in Mark Twain's "The Celebrated Jumping
Frog of Calaveras County." Twain drew upon a floating oral yarn,
one version of which entered print in a sketch, "Frogs Shot without
Powder" in the New York *Spirit of the Times* of May 26, 1855, by

Henry P. Leland, brother of Charles Godfrey Leland.[35] Here is a typical *Spirit* sketch of a Mississippi steamboat yarning session and a tale-within-a-tale. A frog-hunter tells how he placed a handful of shot in one end of a long elder stick he had split to make a trough and then slid the shot down into the mouth of "a thundering big 'Bull-paddy' sunning himself right under a clump of weeds." Bull-paddy caught the lead in his gaping mouth, then caught another shot, and another. When the hunter stepped from behind the grass, the frog could not budge. The hunter picked him up and squeezed the shot out of him to use on another frog.

The Guyuscutus

I N *Huckleberry Finn* (chapters 20 to 23), the self-styled king who is accompanying Huck and Jim on their river journey appears as a prancing, painted, naked figure before a gaping small-town Arkansas audience who have paid to see the Royal Nonesuch. Soon the ticket-buyers realize they have been gulled, but they keep the secret so that the next audience may be similarly deceived. In *Mark Twain at Work,* Bernard DeVoto wrote: "Professor Walter Blair . . . believes that it [the Royal Nonesuch] was related to a widespread folk yarn of the old southwestern frontier which had to do with the fabulous creature known as the gyascutus [*sic*], apparently a very phallic beast."[36] DeVoto had already published, in *Mark Twain in Eruption,* a statement by Mark Twain that he had indeed obtained the account of the Royal Nonesuch from his friend Jim Gillis, with whom he stayed for some months in 1864 and 1865: "In one of my books— *Huckleberry Finn,* I think—I have used one of Jim's impromptu tales, which he called 'The Tragedy of the Burning Shame.' I had to modify it considerably to make it proper for print, and this was a great damage." And Twain laments how mild and pale his printed version seemed alongside Gillis's "extravagant" and "gorgeous" un- printable rendering.[37] The King's performance before his salivating Arkansas voyeurs seems to have been a burlesque phallic dance.[38]

A long, rich comic tradition of oral yarns and humorous newspaper sketches preceded the 1884 unveiling of the Royal Nonesuch by Mark Twain. In his article on the guyuscutus, the commonest name for the escaped critter, B. J. Whiting has traced this history. In print the tradition begins in 1845 and 1846 with four separate but clearly related pieces. George P. Burnham, a Boston journalist who wrote under the sobriquet of "The Young 'Un," contributed two of them. The first, a slight anecdote titled "He Wanted to See the Animal," recounted the misadventure of a yokel come to Boston on the Fourth of July who mistook a sign over a magazine office, Littell's Living Age, for an advertisement of a strange beast on exhibit inside, and created a commotion by insisting on seeing the show. A wag attached some lighted firecrackers to the greenhorn's coat, and as they popped another hanger-on shouted, "Look out! *The crittur's loose.*" Off dashed the countryman to the depot, his coattails streaming, and jumped on a train pulling out of the station.[39]

The germ of the yarn is here, but Burnham in a loosely related variant that he wrote about the same time presented the classic form of what might be called "The Crittur Is Loose" comic anecdote. He himself titled it "Raising the Wind" and printed it in the New York *Spirit of the Times* for October 4, 1845, as follows:

> A good story is told by somebody—we don't recollect who—of a couple Yankees who chanced to be travelling at the South, and had run short of funds. Out of "tin," and out at the toes, they hit upon the following expedient to raise the rhino.
>
> By dint of address they contrived to come it over the printer, and procured a quantity of hand-bills, giving notice to the denizens of the town where they were stopping, that "*a monster* Guyuscutus," of the genus "*humm*," would be exhibited on the following day, at a certain place—admittance 25 cents, children half price. A curtain was obtained, which was drawn across one end of the apartment where the show was to come off, and the time having arrived, one of the worthy pair performed the part of doorkeeper and receiver-general, while his companion in sin was busy behind the screen (which was so arranged as to prevent discoveries) where he kept up an incessant and most unearthly moaning, while the company were entering and being seated. The hour having at last arrived for the show to commence, the doorkeeper left his post, and marching across the hall, which was crowded with men, women and children, he disappeared behind the curtain. Immediately after his exit a terrific howling, barking, and chaffering commenced, in the midst of which the

clattering of chains and a heavy fall or two, were distinctly heard. A terrific struggle appeared to be going on behind the green baize, and an occasional "Oh! ah—hold hard, Jim"—"hit him on the head"—"that's it"—"no it isn't," etc., were heard for some minutes by the audience in front, who by this time had become greatly excited, and not a little alarmed. Amidst the call for the "manager" the exclamations were heard—"he'll break his chains"—*"there he goes!"*—and the doorkeeper rushes from behind the scenes, hatless and breathless, his hair on end, while he shouts at the top of his lungs—"Save yourselves, gentlemen! Save your children! *The Guyuscutus is loose!"*

It needs hardly to be added that the immediate rush for the door was "immense," and that in the *melee,* the overturning of chairs and settees—the shrieks of the women, and the yelling of the children, our Yankees mizzle—while the audience, upon recovering their feet and their senses, only learn, too late, that the "proprietors" of the exhibition have sloped, and that, individually and collectively—*they had been done brown!"*[40]

Subsequent variants extending for more than a century, and no doubt still recoverable, confirm the basic elements of this folktale about a sell: the pair of sharpers who announce the capture of a strange monster, sell tickets to exhibit it to a gullible crowd, create a great commotion behind the scenes, cry out that the crittur is loose, panic the crowd into leaving, and abscond with their take. A version in the *Knickerbocker* in 1846 places six out of pocket Yankees in a Georgia town, and has one rush out, distraught and dishevelled, to cry to the expectant audience, "Ladies and gentlemen! Leave the house immediately! Save yourselves! THE GYANOUSA AM LOOSE!" The same year an Oregonian paper, the *Spectator,* featured a front page story, "The Guiaskuitus" [*sic*] with the same ending, "Save yourselves the Guiaskuitis is loose." In *Harper's New Monthly Magazine* in 1853, from the Editor's Drawer, appeared a particularly impressive version that joined the Guyanosa with another favorite American myth-beast, here called the Prock. A single rogue, sometime clock peddler, schoolkeeper, dentist, and lecturer on phrenology, perpetrates the hoax in a western state, where after his lecture he offered to exhibit two remarkable creatures "that had been caught among the sublime fastnesses of the Rocky Mountains." One was the dangerous Guyanosa, captured by forty hunters with lassos after a four-day chase, and the other the Prock, a grazing animal of the mountainside, possessed of one short hindleg and one short foreleg for convenience in browsing on slopes, whom hunters caught by heading him around so that his long legs stood on the uphill side, whereupon he toppled over helplessly. On the right of the exhibit, after the usual clanking of chains and unearthly shrieks behind the curtain, the exhibitor burst forth shouting, "Save yourselves! The Guyanosa has broken loose, and he has already killed the Prock." Abraham Lincoln is credited with knowing about the telling the Giascutis [sic] tale to Seward, in an 1864 publication of the *Letters of Major Jack Downing, of the Downingsville Militia,* imitative of Seba Smith's Jack Downing. In Lincoln's tale-within-the-tale, he gives away the sell by revealing that one of the Yankees out West was playing Giascutis, growling and rattling his chains behind a curtain. His companion told the people how the monster had killed ten men, two boys, and five horses before he was caught. After the climactic "The Giascutis is loose, Run! run! run!" ending the yarn, Lincoln likens the Merrimac, which sends tugboats and steamers scampering, to the Giascutis.

In the Royal Nonesuch episode in *Huckleberry Finn,* the Duke and the Dauphin do not cry out that the Nonesuch is loose, but make a surreptitious exit on the third night when the townsfolk come armed with rotten eggs and cabbages. And they advertise a thrilling tragedy, "The King's Cameleopard or The Royal Nonesuch!!!" denying admittance to women and children. And the King does perform on all fours, briefly. So the sell varies from the standard formula.

Another mid-nineteenth century reference to both the guyascutus and the prock occurs in the San Francisco *Herald* of December 10, 1855, by the humorist George H. Derby, better known as John Phoenix and Squibob, in a sketch on "The Natural History of Oregon." Under the persona of a Dr. Herman Ellenbogen, Derby describes the quyascutus as a kind of gigantic sloth but harmless; hence the "popular expression of alarm, 'The guyuscutus is loose,' " is unfounded. In a later issue of the paper Dr. Ellenbogen describes in detail a fragment of the heavy bone shield that covered the creature.

Under other names the dreaded beast has continued to frighten away curious customers. In Chillicothe, Ohio, in the 1890s, according to the volume on *Chillicothe and Ross County* in the American Guide Series (1938), one Dan Shriner, a printer, hired a hall and sold tickets to citizens to see the "sky foogle," only to burst upon the stage crying, "Run for your lives, the terrible sky foogle has escaped."[41] Vance Randolph devotes five pages to the gowrow in *We Always Lie to Strangers* (1951). According to reports the gowrow resembled a lizard but grew to twenty feet in length, with great tusks, and was hatched from eggs the size of beer kegs. It inhabited caverns and devoured numbers of domestic animals. A traveling salesman named William Miller and his posse once discovered the lair of a gowrow, according to a newspaper story, and awaited its return. "Presently the earth swayed as if another earthquake were taking place. The waters of the lake began to splash and roar like the movement of the ocean waves. . . ." They did kill the creature, and described it as an enormous pachyderm. A resident of Mena, Arkansas, told Randolph a long story about a Missourian who bragged of capturing a gowrow by feeding it a wagonload of dried apples, which swelled so that the creature could not squeeze back into its burrow. The chap charged viewers twenty-five cents to see the gowrow chained in a tent, in front of which stood a painting of the animal dining on a family of cotton farmers. A roar, followed by the sound of shots and chains clanking was heard from backstage and the showman, bloodied and tattered, rushed out shouting, "Run for your lives, the gowrow has broke loose." Part of the tent collapsed; women screamed; and the crowd lit out.[42]

The Guascutus [*sic*], also called "the Stone-eating Guascutus," turns up in Charles E. Brown's *Paul Bunyan Natural History* (1935) but bears no relationship, other than its name and possibly its fearsome characteristics, to the "critter is loose" tradition:

> This sordid beast has been described as "about the size of a white-tailed deer. Has ears like a rabbit and teeth like a mountain lion. It has telescopic legs which enables it to easily graze on hills. It has a long tail which it wraps around rocks when its legs fail to telescope together. It feeds on rocks and lichens, the rocks enabling it to digest the tough and leathery lichens. It is never seen except after a case of snake-bite."[43]

Another instance of a giasticutus [*sic*] unconnected with the hoax surfaces in the Ozarks in the form of a huge bird of prey, with a wingspread of fifty feet, which swooped down and carried off cattle in its boat-sized beak. A college professor in Missouri claimed that he had heard a farmer's story about a black feather fourteen feet long with a quill as thick as a man's leg, which the farmer had found in his pasture, and which presumably came from the giasticutus. According to Randolph, some country people believed in the existence of the giasticutus, and others thought that Mark Twain or Eugene Field might have launched the tale.[44]

From "Raising the Wind" through the Royal Nonesuch to the Gowrow, we note that the guyuscutus hoax endures as an oral tale. Burnham begins, "A good story is told. . . ." Twain recollects, "As Jim told it . . . I think it was one of the most outrageously funny things I have ever listened to." Vance Randolph writes, "A gentleman at Mena, Arkansas, told me a long story. . . ."

THREE

The Sidehill Dodger

*M*OST widely reported of all the fearsome critters in American comic mythology—although unaccountably omitted by Cox—is the sidehill dodger, also called the sidehill hoofer, sidehill wowser, sidehill winder, and the gwinter, guyiscutus [*sic*], prock, yamhill lunkus, wampus cat, and rackabore.[45] Baughman assigns a new type 1913 to "Lie: the side-hill beast" (Motif X1381) and cites testimonies from observers in six states from Maine to Texas, as well as related motifs of men and conventional animals possessing short legs on one side. An early example of the sidehill beast bears yet another name, the haggletopelter, and surfaces in a longish yarn printed in the New York *Spirit of the Times* for September 27, 1856 (volume 26, p. 392), where I encountered it when doing research for my doctoral dissertation. Titled "A Marvellous Hunting Story" and postmarked from Ampersand Pond, New York, the sketch conforms to the familiar formulas adopted by *Spirit* correspondents. The writer begins in literary style with a vignette of his fisherman's cabin on a granite bluff overlooking a marsh deep in the wilderness. Soon he mentions his guide, who "is prone to relate marvellous tales of 'olden time.' " Now the idiom changes as the guide spins his hunting tale of setting out after deer with Heck, his reliable hound dog, whose "hoot was the forerunner of death." But on this day Heck lay down by a fresh scent and wouldn't budge, until his owner loosed him:

> He gave one bound, then a terrible yell, and entered a thicket of white birch; such a crackling you never heard as was made when that varmint started from his cover! Now, don't laugh; between you and I that was a critter as was a critter, something between a wolf and a deer, with a long bushy tail, no horns, and in color resembling a Col. Baker's mully cow. You see I was used to the woods, and thought I'd seen everything in 'em, but here was a specimen of antiquity for you, a real live specimen.

Details of the chase follow; the hunter gets a bead on the creature and shoots him through the heart:

> Well, you won't believe me, now, when I tell you that creetur had two short legs on one side, and two long ones on the other. . . . Just then up came Cutler [the guide's hunting companion].
> 'My God! Liars, what have you got here?' says he.
> 'There you are into me about a foot,' said I.
> He pulled him over, looked at his two short legs on the up hill side, then his long legs. 'Well,' says he, 'that is a Haggletopelter, made specially for running round side hills. Ah! yes,' he continued, 'this calls up recollections of my poor old father. He caught one on Round Hill, many years since. You see he was after blackberries, when he discovered this singular critter as he started from a thicket of dwarf pines, and gave chase, but found soon 'twas no use, as he kept round the hill ahead of him just in sight; but the old man knew too much for him. He turned round and headed him off, got his long legs on the up hill side, so the varmint rolled over, and he caught him: forget what become of him, I was so young at the time.'[46]

This text, which precedes by half a century the next known reference to the sidehill beast, contains the basic motifs found in later variants: the unusual appearance (a trait common to all fearsome critters); the uneven legs enabling the animal to travel around hills; and its capture by the stratagem of the hunter turning him wrong way around the hill [an episode to which Baughman assigns motif X1381(ca)]. To fit in these several elements the anonymous *Spirit* correspondent has recourse to two separate haggletopelter encounters: one, a hunting story in the frontier vein of bear, deer, and coon chases which conventionally end with shooting the quarry; the other, a chance meeting on a hill, the proper habitat of the sidehill beast, where it can be captured by the hunter causing it to reverse its direction. The writer places a tale-within-a-tale-within-a-tale to cover these points, and he may well have combined two haggleto-pelter oral yarns into his single written narrative.

A lumberjack tale teller sitting in the deacon seat of a bunkhouse relates the genesis of the sidehill beast in Lake Shore Kearney's 1928 book *The Hodag, And other Tales of the Logging Camps.* Although Kearney employs a literary style, even in the presumably oral texts ("the verdure was prolific with beautiful, flowering plants") he fully recognized the storytelling context and describes with ethnographic detail the after-supper institution of the deacon seat. In this milieu he introduces storytelling entertainers and their tales, the first being Mike Dutton from County Wicklow, Ireland, who yarns about "The Sidehill Gouger." As Mike tells it, a long-haired sturdy breed of horses shipped from the mountains of Wicklow replaced oxen in tilling the Wisconsin soil. A hardy stock, known as gougers, they easily withstood the rugged northern Wisconsin winters and accommodated to side hills by developing inside legs four inches shorter than the outside ones. The female gouger lays eggs, and a celebrated trainer and breeder of sidehill gougers, Jimmie Killtime of Glendale Hill, will provide information on their habits upon request.[47]

Gene Shepard, whose hoax of the hodag gave Kearney the title for his book, also yarned about the sidehill beast to attentive listeners, one of whom has left this depiction of Shepard performing:

> "I knew Shepard well, I can see him now sitting in the chair, with one leg crossed over the other, with the upright foot tossing back and forth as he talked.
>
> " 'Gene' was a heavy man with a happy, round face which reflected his thoughts as he related his yarns. I have heard him repeat stories, but they were never the same as the original telling. Always he added new particulars and amplified with greater details of astonishment the story at each unfolding.
>
> "I think more of the fascinating episodes in Bunyan tales originated with 'Gene' Shepard than in any other mind. One of the most gripping was the story of the side hill gouger whose right leg was only one-third as long as his left, so he had to go clear around the mountain to get home. Shepard may have obtained the original idea from some other lumberjack, but the listener

would never recognize the creation after Shepard's second telling, so marvelous were the circumstances supplied."[48]

In Ozark country Vance Randolph heard "backwoods yarn-
spinners talk about the side-hill hoofer." Looking like a calf-sized
beaver, it lived in a hillside burrow and always ran around the hill
in the same direction. On level ground it could not run or even walk.
Female hoofers lay bucket-size eggs, one of which made a breakfast
for twenty-five men. Two grabhook claws on a hoofer's tail enable it
to hang on the edge of a ridge and rest its uneven legs. Another
version likens the hoofer to a kangaroo built sideways. One narrator
defines two species, the clockwise and the anti-clockwise travelers,
who clash in a terrible fight when they meet head-on, since neither
can yield, but can only move forward in long gradual curves around
the mountain if they wish to change level. A man attacked by a
hoofer need only walk directly uphill or downhill a few steps. If a
hoofer falls off a hillside, it lies on its side screaming and dies of
starvation. Randolph heard of a hollow full of hoofer bones in Marion County, Arkansas. He also heard of tales about the side-hill
slicker and the side-hill walloper but could not run them down.
    The baldknob buzzard, a giant vulture once frequently seen in
White County, Arkansas, resembled the side-hill hoofer in possessing only one functioning wing; hence it flew in one direction only
from left to right around hilltops.[49]
    Of all the fanciful creatures in United States folklore the sidehill
beast proves the most ubiquitous. He is reported continuously from
1840, cited as *prock* in the *Dictionary of American English*, up to
the present, and across the country from Maine to California. His
constant feature of the shorter uphill legs stabilizes the tradition,
but various reporters add special twists. Skinner, in Maine, states
that the fat of the side-hill winder cures the diseases (caused by the
mischievous will-am-alone) of hard-drinking lumberjacks, but eating the winder's flesh ensures a "hard and sudden death."[50] Brown
in Wisconsin considers the wampus cat harmless but asserts that its
"very strange antics frightened many a lumberjack into fits."[51] In
Texas an elaborate history furnished by A. W. Penn, in an article
titled "Tall Tales for the Tenderfeet,"[52] recounts how an animal
known as the ornithryncodiplodicus grazed around his one propri-
etary hill and developed shorter uphill legs: "Such a disproportion

in anatomy further distempered the ornithryncodiplodicusical disposition." The peaceful grazer evolved into a ferocious predator and mangled natives who came within his limited reach. To counteract its charge, a smiling frontiersman would proceed on his way until the beast had approached within exactly two steps of him and then stop two paces downhill, whereupon the ornithryncodiplodicus wheeled, turned, tottered and fell screaming into the abyss below. The colony has thinned out, in consequence of the above strategy, and also of the fatal combats that ensued when a clockwise met a counterclockwise species on the same hill. In time the natives substituted the name "mountain stem-winder" for the more formal appellation of the creature. In *Tall Tales from Texas,* Mody Boatright adapted Penn's material, without specific credit, to a tale-telling session between veteran cowboys and a new hand but changed the name of the animal to the gwinter. The old hands tell of a hunting party that set out after a gwinter for a $50,000 price offered by Barnum and Bailey. By pairing in shifts they chased the gwinter higher and higher up the mountain to the top, when it turned itself inside out and ran down the other way.[53] Similarly Nebraska and Kansas natives tell how the Sand-Hill Dodger eluded a cowboy who tried to rope it, thinking that he could corner the critter when it ran out of the hills. But the Dodger swallowed its nose, turned inside out, and headed in the opposite direction with its short legs still on the uphill slope.[54] In California the creature appears under the name of the sidehill guano, and according to a story widespread in the Sierra and the West was a small, lemming-like animal that lived on the steep side of Lembert Dome, Tuolumne Meadows, and other places. It fed on lichens facing the wind, which blew from the west, and consequently its legs on the uphill side became shorter than those on the downhill side. One day the wind shifted to the east, and the starving guanos, unable to eat, tried to turn around to face the wind, lost their balance, and fell to their death. Hence they are now extinct.[55] In a New York lumbercamp a newcomer hunted the Side Hill Jinx, which the old woodsmen told him looked like a fox save that its shorter left legs enabled it to run around sidehills.[56]

In his *Fearsome Critters* Tryon presents some new aspects of the Side-Hill Gouger. Among the variant names he mentions "Gyascutus," a unique instance, in my knowledge, of this merger. Within his description he inserts an oral text from Bill Ericsson of North Haven, Maine, explaining the why and how of the Gougers' westward migration from New England:

> It seems that the Gouger population was getting too thick. There warn't enough food to go around, and somebody just had to move out. A pair of these ambitious little varmints, one orthodox, one abnormal-legged, got together and decided to strike out for a new location. Of course they could navigate on the hillsides and slopes all right; but they knew mighty well they'd bog down on the flats, so when they struck level going they just leaned against each other with the longer legs outermost, sort of like a pair of drunks going home from town.[57]

Thus did Gouger colonies form in the West. Tryon also speaks of fossil remains of extinct Gouger colonies in northwestern Nebraska, of a subspecies in West Virginia whose nigh side sports a beautifully tanned hide from brushing against the steep slopes, and hence fetches a high price in leather goods stores; of another and larger subspecies in Oregon, the Yamhill Lunkers, with reversible legs, which had been broken for farm work; and he reports the comment that "a Side-Hill Gouger is jest a burrowin' buffalo, sized down and growed crooked."[58]

Imaginary animals entered into the Paul Bunyan pseudo-legends, and several authors incorporated the sidehill beast into their chronicles. Esther Shephard in her *Paul Bunyan* devotes a chapter to "The Pyramid Forty" and Paul's logging operations on a side hill. The hen sidehill dodger laid square eggs to keep them from rolling out of the nest, but one once laid her eggs wrong side to and the dodger chicks came out of the shell with their long legs on the uphill side and all rolled down to the river and drowned. Also on the Pyramid Forty the Pinnacle Grouse flew round and round on her one big wing arching the tip of the pyramid.[59]

Besides the fanciful sidehill beast, a number of domestic animals and man himself grow uneven legs because they live and work on slopes. In his index Baughman cites cattle, mules, goats, pigs, and chickens with uneven legs, and gives half a dozen references to a man with one short leg.[60] In my research for *Jonathan Draws the Long Bow,* I uncovered a humorous newspaper sketch of 1841, labeled "An Original Character," that portrayed a Vermont rustic, "a tall rawboned, overgrown, lantern-jawed" youth digging potatoes.

The traveler from the city engages this Jonathan in conversation, and the following exchange ensues:

> "Pray tell me how it happens that one of your legs is shorter than the other?"
>
> "I never 'lows any body to meddle with my grass tanglers, mistur; but seein' it is you, I'll tell ye. I was born so at my tickler request, so that when I hold a plough, I can go with one foot in the furrer, and t'other on land, and not lop over; besides, it is very convenient when I mow round a side hill."[61]

In 1951 Vance Randolph retold aspersions he had heard, even from the governor of Arkansas, that hillbillies in Missouri and Arkansas—depending on the state the speaker comes from—limp on level ground because one leg is shorter than the other from adapting to the rugged terrain.[62]

FOUR

The Hugag

A lengthy history lies behind the first beast to greet the reader of Cox's *Fearsome Creatures of the Lumberwoods*, the hugag, a moose-like quadruped noted for its jointless legs and pendulous upper lip that prevents it from grazing. Cox notes:

> It is reported to keep going all day long, browsing on twigs, flopping its lip around trees, and stripping bark as occasion offers, and at night, since it cannot lie down, it leans against a tree, bracing its hind legs and marking time with its front ones. The most successful hugag hunters have adopted the practice of notching trees so that they are almost ready to fall, and when the hugag leans up against one both the tree and the animal come down. In its helpless condition it is then easily dispatched. The last one killed, so far as known, was on Turtle River, in northern Minnesota, where a young one, weighing 1,800 pounds, was found stuck in the mud. It was knocked in the head by Mike Flynn, of Cass Lake.[63]

In a well-documented article Horace Beck has traced the antiquity of the belief in "The Animal That Cannot Lie Down."[64] Aristotle, in the fourth century B.C., rejected the notion that an elephant cannot bend his legs or sit; but Julius Caesar, in his *Commentaries* on his expedition to Gaul (6th Book, Chapter 27), reported an elk

36

incapable of lying down, in language very similar to the words of Cox:

> There are also animals that are called elks. The shape of these, and the varied color of their skins, are much like does, but in size they surpass them a little and are destitute of horns, and have legs without joints and ligatures; nor do they lie down for the purpose of rest, nor, if they have been thrown down by any accident can they raise or lift themselves up. Trees serve as beds to them; they lean themselves against them, and thus reclining only slightly they take their rest. When the huntsmen have discovered . . . whither they are accustomed to betake themselves they either undermine all the trees at the roots or cut into them so far that the upper part of the trees may appear to be left standing. When they have leant upon them, they knock down by their weight the unsupported trees, and fall down themselves among them.[65]

With authority such as this, the animal that could not lie down became a fixture in medieval bestiaries and surfaced in colonial America among other fauna subject to vulgar errors and travelers' large stories. Indians beyond the Mississippi avowed "that their Contry has Many very large Horses in it which never lyes down to Sleep but leans against a Tree for that purpose," according to a traveler's journal entry in 1761.[66]

Tryon includes the hugag but adds to Cox's version such touches as: "Instead of hair he wears pine needles; and a steady diet of pine knots makes the pitch ooze constantly from his pores."[67] Tryon's illustration depicts not the animal but one of his "sleep-trees" leaning to the right and large hoofprints leading to a shack tilted the other way.

In Schwartz's *Kickle Snifters,* the illustrator shows a sad-looking hugag leaning stiffly on his hind feet against a tilted outhouse, while on the facing page a tilted house, tree, and fence indicate the hugag has passed that way.[68]

FIVE

The Hodag

*O*NE wonders what corroborating testimony supports the existence in tradition of Cox's beasts. In the case of the hodag, testimonials do exist. Cox likens the hodag to the rhinoceros, from descriptions given by woodsmen in Wisconsin and Minnesota, and emphasizes "a large spade-shaped boney growth, with peculiar phalanges, extending up in front of the eye, so that he can only see straight up." His only food is the porcupine; on sighting one in the branches of a spruce tree he spades around the roots, rams the tottering tree, straddles the trunk, and crushes and devours the porcupine head first. In the winter the hodag covers himself with pitch bark, rolls himself into a cover of dead leaves, and lies thus encased until the spring thaws.[69] Although Cox wrote at a period closest in time to the events that publicized the hodag in Wisconsin, his version differs wholly from the traditions that subsequently gained currency. Cox identified the hodag as *nasobatilus hystrivoratus* and Kearney as *bovien spirituallis.*

In 1928 Luke Sylvester Kearney, who used his sobriquet Lake Shore Kearney on the title page, printed in Wausau, Wisconsin, a book of 158 pages titled *The Hodag,* with a subtitle "And Other Tales of the Logging Camps." The author presented tales and poems from the "Golden Lumbering Days" in the northern Wisconsin woods at the turn of the century, in a volume full of interest to the folklorist. Kearney juxtaposed a long verse narrative, "The Round River Drive" by E. S. Shepard, containing early Paul Bunyan tales, woods poems composed by William N. Allen under his pen name Shan. T. Boy, and a clutch of yarns told by named and described tellers in the deacon seat of a lumber camp. These ten tall tales involve fearsome critters, a very strong hero, and Scandinavian dialect recitals, and in their oral frame setting and familiar themes persuade the folklorist of their traditionality.

The jacket cover depicts the hodag stamping on two pine trees, snorting two streams from the nostrils in its bulldog face, and startling the observer with the horns on its head and along its back and curved tail. An eight-page account, not set within the deacon seat backdrop, deals with "The Hodag" from a perspective unlike that of later Wisconsin writers on the monster. Kearney begins with the patient ox that drew the logs from the forest to the river landings and endured the invective of the ox skinners in various nationalities who goaded and cursed him into moving the heavy loads. Oxen lasted usually six years at this drudgery and then were cremated by the lumberjacks under a huge brush pile, continuously replenished for seven years, to cleanse from their remains the taint of accumulated profanity. But from one such pile of ashes emerged a mystical animal, the hodag, whom Eugene Shepard, a naturalist strolling through the woods, first discovered, to his amazement. This is the creature he beheld:

> The animal's back resembled that of a dinosaur, and his tail, which extended to an enormous length, had a spearlike end. Sharp spines, one and a half feet apart, lined the spinal column. The legs were short and massive and the claws were thick and curved, denoting great strength. The broad, furrowed forehead was covered with coarse, shaggy hair and bore two large horns. From the broad, muscular mouth, sharp, glistening white teeth protruded.[70]

The swish of this beast's tail made the earth tremble, and the exhalation of his breath polluted the air. Shepard hiked back to town, consulted the Ancient Order of the Reveeting Society, and enlisted a courageous crew to dig a huge pit fifty feet wide and thirty feet deep, covered with poles, tree limbs, and grass, and baited with an ox led toward the trap by an intrepid athlete. The hodag rushed after the ox and landed in the pit with a great crash. After the capture Mr. Shepard exhibited the hodag and made known to the world from his researches that he had discovered a missing link between the ichthyosaurus, which could devour a hill in a week, and the mylodoan, which pulled down large trees and foraged off their foliage. Kearney notes that Mike Essex of Siberia, Wisconsin, has since maintained the hodag in captivity, and uses a powerful derrick to handle its eggs, which he will ship upon order.

The sage thus abruptly ended, but later in the book in a humorous poem on Calvin Coolidge by Shan. T. Boy titled "I Do Not Choose to Run" occur three verses on the hodag, in the last of which, given below, Coolidge meets the monster:

> When Calvin roams the northern wood,
> On Lake Superior's shore,
> Should meet a Hodag seeking food.
> And hear his awful roar,
> He'll throw away his fishing rod,
> His reel and fancy gun
> And whisper to himself, "My God,
> I think I choose to run."[71]

In 1935 Charles E. Brown gave more space—25 lines—to the hodag than to any other beast, bird, reptile or fish in his little booklet *Paul Bunyan Natural History*. Brown referred to the creature as the "Black Hodag" and quoted its discoverer, Gene Shepard, as saying that it fed on mud turtles, water snakes and muskrats and, when the opportunity offered, human flesh:

> Mr. Shepard found a cave where one of these hodags lived. With the aid of a few lumberjacks he blocked the entrance with large rocks. Through a small hole left in the barricade he inserted a long pole on the end of which he fastened a sponge soaked in chloroform. The hodag, thus rendered unconscious, was then securely tied and taken to Rhinelander, where a stout cage had been prepared for it. It was exhibited at the Oneida County fair. An admission fee was charged and a quite large sum of money earned. Later Mr. Shepard captured a female hodag with her thirteen eggs. All of these hatched. He taught the young hodags a series of tricks, hoping to exhibit the animals for profit.
>
> This ferocious beast had horns on its head, large bulging eyes, terrible horns and claws. A line of large sharp spikes ran down the ridge of its back and long tail. Colored photographs of it can

be obtained at Rhinelander. The hodag never laid down. It slept leaning against the trunks of trees. It could only be captured by cutting deeply into the trunks of its favorite trees. It was a rare animal of limited distribution.[72]

In this rendition the hodag merges with Cox's hugag, or the animal that can't lie down. Also the capture of the female and her eggs do not appear in other versions.

In 1939 Fred L. Holmes devoted two chapters to Eugene Shepard, titled "Ranconteur of the Bunkhouses," in a volume portraying notable Wisconsin personalities. In his sketch of Shepard, Holmes conveys the sense of a lively personality, "a queer combination of community jester and shrewd businessman,"[73] who lived his span (1854–1923) as a farm laborer and timber cruiser in several areas of Wisconsin, but from 1885 until his death resided in Rhinelander. He indulged in wild practical jokes, a number of which Holmes recounts. Shepard also liked to recite Paul Bunyan tales and to draw sketches of Paul Bunyan's camp, and with his wife he published in 1929 in Tomahawk, Wisconsin, a little book on *Paul Bunyan, His Camp and Wife*. His love of pranks led to his announcement, around 1900, that he had captured a prehistoric monster in the Northern Wisconsin wilds. In Holmes' description: "It was a mythical animal of the bovine species, equipped with six horns on the back, two varicolored blinking eyes, and a ferocious face. When the animal moved, its unearthly groans chilled visitors to the marrow; flames emitted from its nostrils; its eyes leered satirically." Holmes states that Smithsonian scientists came to examine the beast at the Wausau and Antigo county fairs where it loomed menacingly from within a dark tent. Shepard told them it would eat nothing but white bulldogs, and only on Sundays (a motif lacking in Brown). Finally he admitted that a woodcarver had shaped the body, using bull's horns as spikes along the backbone, bear's claws for eyebrows, curved steel spikes for claws, and ox hides for the skin. But he kept playing with the hoax and gathered friends armed with axes and pitchforks to be photographed slaying the monster. Postcards in the hundreds of thousands depicting this scene brought tourists thronging to Rhinelander and Oneida County. Rhinelander's athletic teams called themselves Hodags, and in 1904 Shepard had a palatial riverboat built for him named "The Hodag."[74]

Also in 1939 Tryon's *Fearsome Critters* included a drawing of the hodag that followed closely the image popularized by the Rhine-lander postcards and the jacket cover of Lake Shore Kearney's book, but the text deviates from all other accounts. Tryon states that the hodag had first been reported in Maine and later captured by F. [sic] S. Shepard in Rhinelander, Wisconsin, but then gives him charac-teristics of the Squonk, to wit that he weeps bitterly because of his upsetting appearance. A lady who collected his crystallized tears and strung them into a neck-yoke, thinking them fine amber, spilled a Tom Collins on the necklace, whereupon the lemon juice dissolved them instantly. A pair of lemons suffices to ward off a herd of irate hodags.[75]

In 1941 Curtis MacDougall allotted a page to the hodag in his book *Hoaxes* and reproduced a postcard picture of the creature. He described it as "a beast with the head of a bull, the grinning face of a giant man, thick short legs set off by heavy strong claws, the back of a dinosaur, and a long tail with a spear at the end." Basically MacDougall condensed Kearney's account, which he cites, but he provided some new details. The name "hodag" derived from "horse" and "dog," as the monster exhibited to curious visitors in a dimly lit space was in truth a decorated horse hide stretched over a large dog. Kearney quotes the editor of the Rhinelander *Daily News* and the head of the news bureau at the University of Arkansas, who grew up in Wausaw, Wisconsin, on the attention and publicity given the hodag. Stories in metropolitan newspapers, stuffed replicas dis-played at fairs and in parades, and large photographs adorning sa-loons of the hodag atop a fallen log surrounded by his captors kept his memory green. "Whenever a convention meets at Rhinelander, the fame of the monster lives anew."[76]

In 1962 in *Wisconsin Lore* Robert E. Gard and L. C. Sorden re-printed Kearney's account of the hodag and appended a statement on how Gene Shepard thrilled curiosity-seekers at country fairs throughout Wisconsin with the groaning, blinking, flame-snorting monster until his hoax was revealed. They ascribe the creation of the hodag to a clever woodcarver, the use of oxhides, and Shepard's inspiration. In a note, "More on the Hodag," they add a statement from an informant in Rhinelander that the hodag was captured on February 30 on Section 37 (a township has only 36 sections) and that the acre of ground upon which Shepard had discovered him would soon be moved within the city limits. Thanks to Shepard's invention, Rhinelander is known today as "The Hodag City." Gard and Sorden call Shepard "the greatest trickster of them all" who performed hundreds of pranks, a number of which they report, for nearly forty years in the Rhinelander area, and who decorated letters to friends with drawings of Paul Bunyan's lumber camp located forty miles west of Rhinelander on the Onion River. Shep is pictured as "hulking fellow with a barrel chest . . . the absolute epitome of northwoods humor. . . . Many years have passed since the lumber industry in Wisconsin reached its climax, yet the Gene Shepard influence, the Paul Bunyan influence, is still strong."[77]

In 1969 Walker Wyman set down in his *Mythical Creatures of the North Country* a straightforward narrative concerning "Hodag," with some familiar and some novel details:

> One day when Gene Shepard, a former lumberjack who settled down near Rhinelander, Wisconsin, was walking near his wooded Shangri-la he smelled something strange. It made his nostrils quiver. Then he heard a growl, the like of which he had never before heard. In the brush he saw a terrifying sight, a monster that had the head and body of an ox, but a tail like that of a lizard or an alligator. Along the back were six sharply pointed spines that gave it the appearance of a prehistoric dinosaur. Shepard saw its thick claws and cloven hooves, saw it snort fire, and concluded that where he was just wasn't any place for a man to be.

As Wyman continues the tale, Shepard ran home as fast as his legs could carry him, got out his old encyclopedia to read up on dinosaurs, and concluded that he had seen a prehistoric monster right there in Valas County. Reading further, he learned that these animals wouldn't eat anything but white bulldogs and them only on Sunday. The next day he labored hard digging a deep pit in the area where he had first spied the monster, then placed two white bulldogs in the pit, and left the area for a long and restless night. Early the next morning, Sunday, he returned to the spot, to hear a terrifying howl coming from the pit and small a stench as bad as buzzard meat and skunk perfume combined. He placed the monster in a sturdy cage and headed happily back home, worrying how he could keep this animal alive if it would eat only white bulldogs and them only on Sunday.

Soon the word got around that Shepard had captured a prehistoric animal known as the hodag. The Milwaukee *Journal* sent a reporter up to investigate this great discovery of the scientific world, and it was said that the Smithsonian Institution also sent an investigator out to this remote part of Wisconsin. Shepard decided to capitalize upon the interest and exhibited the hodag at several county fairs:

> There are some who say that the Hodag is a great hoax, but a visit to Rhinelander soon convinces one that the Hodag is very real even today. A replica of it stands at the opening of the Rhinelander Logging Museum and smaller replicas can be purchased inside. The high school athletic teams call themselves "Hodags" and have the reputation of being fierce in competition.
> Only one question remains: if the Hodag was a hoax and never really existed, then why aren't there more white bulldogs throughout the North Country today?[78]

The hodag phenomenon nicely illustrates the interplay of the fearsome critter tall tale, the prehistoric monster hoax, the mock legend, and small-town boosterism in the American style. Eugene Shepard and his contrivance become part of the narrative, and he acquires the status of a trickster-hero sharing the spotlight with his creation, the odoriferous, mysterious hodag.

SIX

Oscar the Turtle: The Beast of 'Busco

A monster turtle supposedly sighted in Churubusco, Indiana, in 1949 put that town on the map and achieved national visibility. In this instance a trained folklorist, John Gutowski, pursuing doctoral studies in folklore at Indiana University and teaching a folklore course at the university campus in Fort Wayne, learned of the turtle affair in nearby Churubusco and wrote up its history and current status in a model dissertation study.

Although the "Beast of 'Busco" soared into extravaganza, its annals commenced on the plane of reality. In February 1949, a farmer named Gale Harris, a God-fearing Nazarene reputed not to smoke, drink, or lie, sighted a great turtle in Fulk Lake located on his farm where he was shingling his roof. The Harris farm lay on the outskirts of Churubusco, a community of fifteen hundred souls fifteen miles northwest of Fort Wayne and indistinguishable from hundreds of other Plainvilles and Main Streets throughout the United States. Fulk Lake did, however, enjoy a local reputation for dangers, mysteries, and strange wildlife, and natives had spoken for half a century of a monstrous creature in its vicinity. Harris believed he had spied Oscar the Turtle with a "shell as big as an old fashioned dining room table" and weighing four to five hundred pounds. Oscar would thus be the largest inland snapping turtle ever seen by man. For the next fortnight farmers and conservationists helped

45

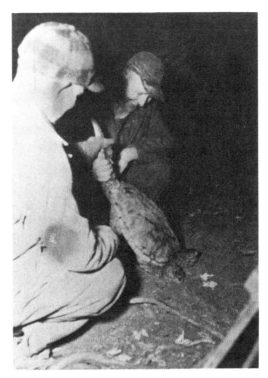

Gale Harris pulling a 52-pound snapping turtle from Fulk Lake.

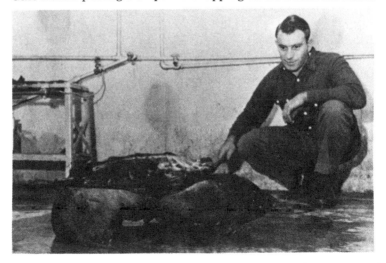

A 100-pound alligator snapper, the alleged "Beast of 'Busco," with its captor, Woodrow Rigsby.

Harris hunt and fish for the turtle. Then on March 7, a paper in the next town, the *Columbia City Post-Mail*, featured a tongue-in-cheek story, "Five Hundred Pound Turtle Would Make Lots of Good Turtle Soup," containing these comments:

> . . . Residents of Eel River Township, Allen-County, have located a 1949 model turtle said to be as big as a car top, a dining room table top or a ten man poker table. . . . Reports have it that a turtling concern from Cincinnati, Ohio has placed a top price of $1800 on the animal, dead or alive. The reptile has been variously described by native residents as "too big to go through a door," "as thick as a sack of clover seed," and "a head as big as a man's." . . . One bystander said, "If Campbell's Soup Company could catch this animal, they could remove 'mock' from their turtle soup label.

The wire services and radio broadcasters picked up the story, and reporters, naturalists, deep sea divers and commercial fishermen descended on Churubusco. For ten months Harris pursued Oscar with "harpoons, shark hooks, dragging hooks, home-made chicken wire and rope nets, home made underwater viewing apparati, centrifugal pumps, tractors, cranes, and beams." But Oscar eluded every stratagem, while Harris twice nearly drowned and suffered temporary blindness. Finally he vowed, "If I have to drain that lake dry to prove I'm telling the truth, I'll do it." Within one day of finishing the two month long draining process Harris took to bed with appendicitis. During his recuperation rains flooded and broke his dams and re-filled the lake. Disheartened and defeated, Harris gave up the quest.

But the joy of the hunt lived on in the carnival spirit that had enveloped Fulk Lake and the annual Turtle Days Festival and commenced in downtown Churubusco in 1950. Merchants and other citizens of Churubusco gaily and profitably identified with Oscar the Turtle. As Gutowski has written, "Souvenir turtles were sold out of every store. The clothing shop reported all but two turtle-neck sweaters out of stock. One restaurant sold more turtle soup in two days than it had sold in a year, after advertising "Best of 'Busco" turtle soup on its windows." Gutowski goes on to list shop window and newspaper advertisements announcing free rifles, radios, ice cream to whoever guessed Oscar's weight to the nearest half ounce, with other come-ons by a realtor, an insurance company, cafe owners, in behalf of "Oscar, The Busco Monster," "the Beast of Busco," and "Our Oscar." Pat's Cafe promised to serve turtleburgers as soon as Oscar was caught. The town newspaper, the Churubusco *Truth,* carried tall tales and elegiac verses in honor of Oscar. A sample tale goes:

> Charlie Horner, the butcher, says that when a mule was used in an attempt to pull the "Fulk Lake monster" from the water, the turtle pulled the mule into the lake—ate him—and came out of the water picking his teeth with a single tree.

Gutowski himself was gulled during his field work by a solemn informant, who volunteered an elaborate account of turtlehunters attempting to pull Oscar from the lake and so effect his capture. At first they tried tractors hooked onto a chain around Oscar, but the machines could not get enough traction. So the hunters resorted to a team of mules. The turtle burrowed down in the mud, and pulled the mules down into the lake. "It ended up that that was the first piece of ass that that turtle had had in over a hundred years!"

In due course hoax turtles, imported from Florida and Missouri or constructed from logs, canvas, and old tires, made their appearance and started new waves of media attention until the righteous Harris punctured the claims. But Oscar's hold on the Churubuscans is secure. An annual festival, replete with turtle races, a Turtle Queen, parades, bands, booths, and all the trappings, pays homage to the one and only Beast of 'Busco.[79]

A sixteen-page booklet printed in September 1978 by the Churubusco Chamber of Commerce displays a cover photograph of a pleasant covered sidewalk and peaceful street scene, with shade trees in the background and a stone replica of a large turtle alongside a potted sapling in the foreground. Beneath the picture a caption reads: CHURUBUSCO, INDIANA, *A Community with a Tradition . . . and a Future!* In the right-hand margin appears the inscription TURTLE TOWN U.S.A. In the lower right-hand corner a sketch of an impish little turtle sporting a sailor's hat contrasts with the stiffness of the stone turtle.

The booklet conveys a comfortable sense of a thriving town that has passed from an agricultural to a suburban phase and offers "the satisfying life of the smaller community" along with "the advantages of big-city employment" in nearby Fort Wayne. A place-name legend explains the choice of Churubusco in 1847 by a pioneer woman seeking to placate a German, an Englishman, and an Irishman who were championing the names of Brunswick, Liverpool and Maloney, respectively. The compromiser suggested Churubusco in honor of the victory won there in the Mexican War by the American army; and the Irishman, who had taken off his coat prepared to do battle, put it on again saying that although he could not pronounce it he would accept the name as a patriotic gesture. Turtle traditions emerge twice in Churubusco's history: first, in the presence of Little Turtle, Chieftain of the Miami Indians who won notable victories in the area; and second, in the annals of Oscar, whose appearance "gained nationwide attention" in 1949 and whose "disappearance is a mystery to this day." The third of three paragraphs devoted to the turtle states: "The saga of Oscar is commemorated each year in Churubusco's four-day 'Turtle Days' celebration, in which a Turtle Queen is crowned and many special events are scheduled." Immediately following comes the sentence: "Today Churubusco is an expanding community, for both homes and industry."

The Jackalope

A creature with the body and legs of the jackrabbit and the head and horns of a small deer, the jackalope made his first appearance in a round-up of American mythical animals only in 1969. Wyman included a description and drawing of the jackalope with unusual quadrupeds from the north country of Wisconsin and Minnesota, and stated that plains animals like the coyote and the jack rabbit had migrated to the northern pineries with the gutting of the great forests. He reported three known specimens: in Augusta, Wisconsin; in Cornucopia on the South Shore of Lake Superior; and in the museum and lumber camp on the North Shore—presumably shot by careless hunters during the deer season. This species he called the "Jack-pine Jackelope, a mythological throwback that defies even the most compctcnt biologists of the region," and notes that it makes "a cry like that of a human" and hums "with the lilt of the old shanty-boy songs that once made the rafters ring in the lumbercamps."[80]

In a footnote Wyman acknowledged the existence of a subspecies from the Great Plains, the Alkali Area Jackalope, but considered as merely conjecture the possibility of its predating the North Country hybrid. Such an attitude would surely infuriate the residents of Douglas, Wyoming, who display an attachment to the jackalope comparable to the affection felt by Churubuscans for Oscar the Tur-

The Jackalope

tle, as this story from the Indianapolis *Star* of December 1, 1977, distributed by the New York Times Service, plainly shows.

TOURISTS LOVE JACKALOPE
Hoax Jacks Up Town's Economy

Douglas, Wyo.—While thousands of hunters roam the West this year in search of big game, few, if any, are lucky enough to catch the legendary jackalope, an animal with a jackrabbit's body and the antlers of a deer.

Although Big Foot, the Loch Ness Monster, and other creatures of disputed existence have gained more scientific attention, residents of this small eastern Wyoming community thought enough of the jackalope to erect an 8-foot statue of it in the middle of town.

There are some persons in Douglas who will insist that the jackalope does, indeed, exist. But Ralph Herrick, a taxidermist here, admits, somewhat reluctantly, that he and his brother, Doug, created the Jackalope in 1934.

One evening when they were late for dinner, they placed a recently-caught rabbit beside a pair of antlers on the floor of the taxidermy shop.

"When we came back, Doug said 'Let's mount it the way it is,' "
Herrick said.

Since that time, Herrick's jackalope trophy business has continued to grow. "Lately, I can't make 'em fast enough," he said.

The Douglas Chamber of Commerce issues thousands of jackalope hunting licenses every year to tourists, and signs on the
highway near here tell motorists to "watch out for the
jackalope."

ALTHOUGH THE creature's fame has spread throughout the
West, Herrick and a South Dakota company are the only two
concerns now producing jackalopes. Herrick's brother stopped
making them more than 25 years ago. Gift shops in town do a
brisk business selling jackalope postcards and other novelty
items.

The jackalope was the main attraction here until discoveries
of vast deposits of uranium, coal, oil and natural gas more than
doubled the town's population to 7,500 in the last three years.
Herrick said his business has grown independently of the town's
new-found prosperity, as persons from around the country began
to hear about the jackalope.

Some parts of this tourist industry have never been very popular, like canned jackalope milk, but Herrick sold more than 165
trophies at up to $35 each last year, and he has already sold more
than that this year.

Tourists who purchase jackalope permits are surprised to learn
they may only hunt the creatures "on the 31st day of June, between the hours of 12 midnight and 2 a.m."

HERRICK SAID he does not know how many of the legends
surrounding the jackalope began, such as the one about the creature's extraordinary ability to imitate the human voice, or the
story that said the first man to see the jackalope "was a trapper
named Roy Ball in 1829."

Actually, the original jackalope was sold 43 years ago to the
late Ball, who put it on display in his La Bonte Hotel here. This
jackalope was stolen from the hotel in September, and the culprit
remains at large.

Two of the favorite sports of Douglas residents are convincing
gullible tourists that the jackalope does exist and reinforcing the
beliefs of those who already think the horned rabbit is real.

The Chamber of Commerce of Douglas, Wyoming, distributes four
jackalope-associated items to inquirers. (1) One is a postcard showing a photograph of the jackalope in a sitting position, its antlers
prominently displayed. On the address side an inscription reads:
"The Jackalope of Douglas, Wyoming" and a short paragraph gives
some "facts" about the animal. A longer description is available on

one side of (2) a "Non-Resident Jackalope Hunting Permit," as follows:

> The Jackalope is perhaps the rarest animal in North America. The strange little fellow defies classification. Were it not for the horns it might be a large rabbit. Were it not for its shape and coloring it might be a species of deer. It is not vicious usually, although coyotes have a fine respect for the sharp menace of its horns. The first white man to see this singular fauna specimen was a trapper named Roy Ball in 1829. When he told of it later he was promptly denounced as a liar. An odd trait of the Jackalope is its ability to imitate the human voice. Cowboys singing to their herds at night have been startled to hear their lonesome melodies repeated faithfully from some nearby hillside. The phantom echo comes from the throat of some Jackalope. They sing only on dark nights before a thunderstorm. Stories that they sometimes get together and sing in chorus is discounted by those who know them best.

The reverse side of this thin slip of paper constitutes the permit proper:

NON-RESIDENT JACKALOPE HUNTING PERMIT   No._____

This permit authorizes _____

of _____, to hunt, pursue and take one (1), one-tailed Jackalope within the boundaries of Converse County, Wyoming, on the 31st day of June, between the hours of 12:00 midnight and 2:00 a.m. only. The holder of the license is hereby attested to be a man of strict temperance and absolute truthfulness, except that in cases where the number of Jackalope he has seen or slain is under investigation, he may occasionally, at his discretion, take such lingual evasion or loud rebuttal as the occasion requires.

WARNING! The laws of the State of Wyoming prohibit the killing of two-tailed Jackalope under any circumstances. Penalty: $1,000 fine and-or sentence of six months residence in

Subscribed and sworn to before me this _____day of _____, 19____.

ADAM LYRE, Chief Licensor.

(Signature of Licensee)   By _____Deputy

(A limited number of these permits may be obtained from the Douglas, Wyoming Chamber of Commerce, for the nominal fee of $1.00)

(3) In addition a four-page leaflet titled "If you Are Curious . . ." above a drawing of the Jackalope, his head facing the reader, and a caption beneath the drawing, "Douglas, Original Home of the Jackalope," gives eight items about Douglas as the "Home" of various attractions, such as the "Wyoming State Pioneer Museum, Over 15,000 Exhibits of The Old West," and of "The Only Jackalope Herd in the World." Pages 2 and 3 contain a little "Map of Douglas Area" indicating twenty-one points of interest, the last of which is the Jackalope Statue in downtown Douglas. Page 4 lists some of the exhibits in the Pioneer Museum. (4) An eight-page colored brochure with photographs of grazing deer, mountain peaks, meadows, lakes, and a fish catch bears the heading "A Warm Western Welcome to Douglas, Wyoming, 'Home of the Jackalope.'" Underneath a photograph shows the large-sized Jackalope statue in the center of town, with a smiling, Stetson-hatted citizen standing alongside, one hand resting on the neck of the Jackalope, whose huge head, rabbit ears, and antlers dwarf the man. Entries in the brochure outline the attractions of the Douglas area in "wonderful Wyoming" and conclude with a paragraph about the jackalope.

EIGHT

The Hoopsnake

SNAKES fascinated the first settlers in North America, and none more so than the horn snake, which John Lawson thus described in 1709 in *A New Voyage to Carolina:*

> Of the horn snakes, I never saw but two that I remember. They are exactly like the rattlesnake in color, but rather lighter. They hiss exactly like a goose when anything approaches them. They strike at their enemy with their tail (and kill whatsoever they wound with it), which is armed at the end with a horny substance, like a cock's spur. This is their weapon.
>
> I have heard it credibly reported, by those who said they were eye-witnesses, that a small locust tree, about the thickness of a man's arm, being struck by one of these snakes at ten o'clock in the morning, then verdant and flourishing, at four in the afternoon was dead, and the leaves red and withered.[81]

Other colonial observers in Pennsylvania, New Jersey, and Virginia confirmed this happening. Writers on colonial natural history reported the horn snake in Pennsylvania striking a tree that died in twenty-four hours and again in New Jersey where it took forty-eight; in Virginia it locked itself onto a musket.[82] An English traveler to Virginia, John Ferdinand Dalziell Smyth, in *A Tour in the United States of America* (published in London in 1784), condemned horn snakes "as the most formidable and direful foes in existence to the human race . . . poisonous and fatal to a degree almost beyond credibility. . . . [Each] has a weapon in his tail, called his sting, of a hard, horney substance, in shape and appearance very much like to a cock's spur . . . if it penetrates the skin, it is inevitable and sudden death." Smyth then repeated the marvel of the snake piercing a young sapling with his horn into the tree's sap, and causing the bark within a few hours to "swell, burst, and peel off," and the tree to perish. Finally he pictured the horn snake's method of attack: "he throws himself into a circle, running rapidly round, advancing like a hoop, with his tail arising and pointing forward in the circle, by which he is always in the ready position of striking. . . . From the above circumstance, peculiar to themselves, they have also derived the appellation of hoop snakes."[83]

Although Smyth asserted that the horned snake crawled on its belly like other snakes when not attacking, the Tory soldier of the American Revolution, Nicholas Cresswell, stated in his journal that it always "tumbles tail over head," but otherwise he concurred on its reputation as the "most venomous Snake that is known," capable of killing a tree with its horn. Cresswell described it as scaley like a fish, black and white on the back, with a small hair in its tail like a cockspur, small horns, and about nine feet long. When disabled, it roared like a calf.[84]

In 1859 in the volume of ante-bellum Southern humor most clearly related to oral storytelling, *Fisher's River (North Carolina) Scenes and Characters,* Harden E. Taliaferro recorded a version of "The Horn-Snake." "Skitt" (his pseudonym) was recollecting incidents from his youth in the Blue Ridge mountains of northwestern North Carolina in the 1820s, and he set down a string of traditional tall tales as told by an old friend and neighbor, Uncle Davy Lane, in mountain dialect. Davy dresses up the time-honored account in his own idiom. While hunting on Round Peak he encounters "one uv the curiousest snakes I uver seen in all my borned days. . . . There it lay on the side uv a steep presserpis, at full length, ten foot long, its tail strait out, right up the presserpis, head big as a sasser, right toards me, eyes red as forked lightnin', lickin' out his forked tongue, and I could no more move than the Ball Rock on Fisher's Peak. But when I seen the stinger in his tail, six inches long and sharp as a needle, stickin' out like a cock's spur, I thought I'd a drapped in my tracks." When a rabbit distracted the snake, Uncle Davy jumped forty feet down the mountain and hid behind a thick white oak tree. The snake caught the end of his tail in his mouth, rolled down the mountain like a hoop, and struck the other side of the tree with his stinger, clean up to his tail. "Of all the hissin' and blowin' that uver you hearn sense you seen daylight, it tuck the lead. Ef there'd a bin forty-nine forges all a-blowin' at once, it couldn't a beat it. He rared and charged, lapped round the tree, spread his mouf and grinned at me orful, puked and spit quarts and quarts of green pisen at me, an' made the ar stink with his nasty breath." Uncle Davy seized his gun Bucksmasher and finally shot the snake between the eyes. "Soon as he were dead as a herrin'; all the leaves was wilted like a fire had gone through its branches." When Uncle Davy passed by three weeks later, the "whole tree was dead as a door-nail."[85]

The frontispiece to *Fisher's River*, labeled "The Horn-Snake," shows a vivid sketch of the coiled snake, his stinger planted in the tree, spitting furiously at a frightened, moonfaced fellow in wool hat and linsey-woolsey dress on the other side of the tree.

In its issue of August 4, 1876, the *Idaho World* carried a story of three hunters in the Hagerman area who beheld hundreds of hoop-snakes with their tails in their mouths rolling down the canyon wall to the river where they unrolled themselves, slid to the edge, and drank. One hunter, William Horton, informed the editor that: "This species of snakes thickens itself a little in front of its point of contact with the earth so as to make itself heavier at this spot than in any other part of its body. As the center of gravity falls in front of the base, the snake revolves in the direction of its 'wad.' "[86]

In 1893 Mary Alicia Owen included several told-for-true hoop-snake experiences in her *Voodoo Tales as Told among the Negroes of the Southwest,* recounted in thick Missouri dialect, save for one transliterated text. Big Angie tells how her brother, riding from his cabin to the store, is thrown when his pony rears at the sight of hoopsnakes. The man continues on foot across Sauk Prairie and espies millions of hoopsnakes rolling every which way and trying to roll on him. He runs like a deer, and they roll after him until darkness comes and the moon rises, but still he runs till daybreak. Suddenly, nearly dead, he thinks to say an *Ave* and a *Pater Noster,* squats and spits. Frightened by the spells the snakes roll away. In midday children see him in the berry patch, lying like a dead man. They tell the adults, who rouse him, and he relates his adventure. Aunt

Mynee questions whether Big Angie's brother had drunk from his jug, and Big Angie indignantly rejects the implication, saying the snakes must have conjured the liquor out of the now empty jug.[87]

In 1896 the prolific writer on American Indian myths, Daniel G. Brinton, reminiscing about his Pennsylvania youth, recalled hearing how the hoopsnake would "take his tail in his mouth, stiffen his body, and revolve like a wheel, with such rapidity that a horse could not overtake him." When pressed for the exact place where it lived, his informants would reply, "In the barr'ns," or "Down Marlan." A confirmed solar mythologist, Brinton pondered whether "this hoopsnake fable was an ancient sun-myth sunk to an ordinary snake story," and mused that the snake with his tail in his mouth often appeared as a symbol of the sun's motion and the flight of time in mythical devices found in both hemispheres. The connection between snakes and the sun, continued Brinton more confidently, could certainly be demonstrated in the notion that the tail of a black snake which has been killed and hung across a fence will vibrate all day until the sun goes down.[88]

In 1896 a collector of New England folklore, Clifton Johnson, duly noted the speed and venom of the hoopsnake and added a new detail to its ferocity. "It is said that when a hoopsnake strikes a man it 'blasts' him. I suppose that means he is paralyzed, turns black, shrivels up, and like enough blows away." Johnson had also heard that if the hoopsnake struck its tail into a wooden object, say a hoe handle, the wood shivered into splinters as if it had been struck by lightning.[89]

Beliefs of black persons in the powers of hoopsnakes can be cited in folklore publications from 1914 to 1928. One such belief linked the coachwhip snake to the hoopsnake in a hybrid serpent which overtook a swift runner and whipped his victim to death with its four-plaited tail. If the human target feigned death to deceive the snake, it thrust the pointed end of its tail into the man's nose to see if he was breathing, or into his ear to puncture the eardrum, causing the victim to cry out in pain, whereupon the reptile tail-whipped him to death.[90] Another notion cautioned against trying to kill a hoopsnake with a stick, "because de pison run up yo arm an kill you."[91] Newbell N. Puckett in his *Folk Beliefs of the Southern Negro* (1926) assembled various of these conceptions, such as the idea that hoopsnakes will stand up on the tip of their tail and whistle like a man; if he whistles back they will respond and thus lead him to his death.[92] To escape from a hoopsnake never run straight, as it cannot turn without "quirling" (coiling).[93] In a Mississippi anecdote of the poisoned tree, the teller, Ai' Betsey, recommends as an antidote for hoopsnake bite splitting a live black chicken open and slapping it on the bite; as the chicken draws the poison out it will turn bright green.[94]

Among the yarns delivered from the deacon seat in Lake Shore Kearney's *The Hodag,* a logger named Patrick Sheeron told two in mannered speech under the heading "The Hoop Snake." As a lad driving an ox team hauling a lumber wagon, a hoopsnake rolled in his path and struck the wagon tongue with its tail. The impact killed the snake instantly, but the tongue swelled so greatly that the ring of the yoke burst and struck and killed both oxen in their tracks. The other yarn, which Sheeron also told as a personally observed experience, involved a poor farmer, Bill Peachy, whose prized hoe handle, made of black mahogany, swelled into a log two feet thick after a hoopsnake had struck it with its fangs. Peachy and young Sheeron and a powerful neighbor called Cock Robin loaded the still swelling hoe handle onto a wagon, and with great exertion the ox team pulled it to the sawmill run by Sheeron's father. "And gentlemen, that hoe handle cut seven thousand feet of the finest black mahogany lumber you ever saw, giving this family, the company for which we work, their start in the lumber business."[95]

A Texas banker wrote down in 1930 an account of a snake-yarning session among a crowd of farmers gathered on Saturday night at Pap Dugan's store. Shorty Stubbs climaxed the session "with his famous hoop snake experience." According to Shorty, the hoopsnake far eclipsed other snakes in its deadliness, for while the rattlesnake sounded a warning, and the copperhead and moccasin moved like snails, "a hoop snake, now, he comes like the wind—and makes no more racket than a rubber-tired bicycle. . . . on the end of his tail he has a horn or spike sorter like a rooster's spur about four or five inches long and sharp as a needle. About a half inch from the sharp end is a little valve-like opening through which he shoots his pison. . . . As soon as he decides what animal he is going to tackle he curls himself into a regular hoop . . . and takes his tail in his mouth and rises up just like an old-fashioned bicycle casing and here he comes like hell a-beating tan bark." Shorty then went on to relate the time back in Tennessee when he was out squirrel hunting and had stopped under a wild plum tree, when a hoopsnake rolled toward him; the snake drove his spike with his sharp tail foremost at Shorty "with a powerful penetrating force," and hit the tree into whose branches Shortly had desperately jumped. "Well, boys, I knew he had poisoned that tree, for before I could get to the ground I see the leaves wilting and curling up, and the plums begin to shrivel up and fall off right now."

Old Luke Larkin then told of a hoopsnake back in Alabama in '87 that struck his hoe handle while he was hoeing a cotton row. "That snake socked his horn into that seasoned ash handle and, believe me or not—it was an eye hoe—the old kind—that hoe handle swelled up and bust out of the hoe before I could get to the house."[96]

In 1931 Lowell Thomas, the "Radio Voice of *The Literary Digest,*" in his *Tall Stories* assigned the hoopsnake "an honorable place in the legendry of the Great American Whopper," and offered two tales of a pitch fork handle and a wagon tongue that swelled from a hoopsnake's sting.[97]

In 1934 Ralph Steele Boggs reprinted with commentary the folktale texts from Taliaferro's *Fisher's River Scenes,* including Uncle Davy Lane's hoopsnake story, and mentioned five counties in North Carolina where he himself had heard similar hoopsnake experiences. Boggs also noted that Mark Twain referred to hoopsnakes in his *Autobiography.*[98]

In 1937 Chapman J. Milling raised the question, "Is the Serpent Tale an Indian Survival?" concerning popular beliefs attached to the coachwhip snake, the jointsnake, and the hoopsnake. He set down an archetypal hoopsnake story as he had heard it in South Carolina, and pointed out that the single element of fact in this legend of *Farancia abacura* was the possession by the hoopsnake of a short spine which, however, was "neither erect like a horn nor retractable like a sting." Milling cited Raymond Ditmars, the well known herpetologist, as saying that *Farancia abacura* is a slow-moving, degenerate species. So whence the legend? John Lawson's 1714 account from North Carolina of the horn snake, and similar reports of 1779 and 1859 from South Carolina, all seem to Milling to suggest an Indian origin for this and other snake stories.[99]

With the initiation of the *Hoosier Folklore Bulletin* in 1942 by Herbert Halpert, folklorists could refer to exact texts and meaty comparative references rather than paraphrases, synopses, or fanciful reconstructions, and as proof of its ubiquity "The Poisonous Hoopsnake" made its appearance in the first three issues with versions set in Gary, Indiana, Jefferson County, Kentucky, and Sturgis, Michigan.[100] In *Hoosier Folklore,* the successor to *Hoosier Folklore Bulletin,* the hoopsnake surfaced in Iowa, New Mexico, and West Virginia in 1946, 1947, and 1948.[101] The seven texts all deal with the lethal sting of the hoopsnake as it strikes a wagon tongue, a man's peg-leg, cattle, trees, and a wagon axle. Peg-Leg Pete used an ax to chop three bushels of kindling and two hard piney knots from his swollen wooden limb before it subsided.[102] In an unusual variant a boy and a girl climb an apple tree to escape the hoopsnake, which keeps rolling around the tree, until the hungry children pick an apple to eat and fall dead from the tree at the first bite.[103]

In 1951 the *Journal of American Folklore* carried "Another Hoopsnake Story," reported from a small mountain town in southwestern West Virginia. A hoopsnake rolled down a hill chasing a man and struck an ax handle, which swelled into a huge log. A native built a house from the lumber, but after a while it shrank to the size of the ax, still keeping the shape of a house, as the power of the poison wore off.[104]

"The legend of the hoop snake is common in the Ozark country," wrote Vance Randolph in 1951, and he proceeded to set forth a swatch of hoop snake stories.[105] In one account the hoopsnake's stinger touched a woman's dress, and when she washed the dress the next day the venom "turned three tubs of wash water plumb green." In another, told in the Arkansas state guidebook, a man escaped from a hoopsnake, but fifteen years later he chopped down for firewood the tree killed by the snake's stinger, stuck a splinter in his mouth for a toothpick, and died before sundown. As one would expect, belief tales yield to tall tales, and Randolph speaks of wagon-tongues, hoe handles, rifle muzzles, and even flint boulders that swelled prodigiously when struck by a hoopsnake. The owner of a swollen wagon tongue trimmed it back to size and found he had seven ricks of cordwood and a haystack of chips left over. In another version a small sprout swelled into an enormous tree, which a hill-man sawed into boards for a chicken house, but after he painted it the building shrank to the size of a bird box; the turpentine in the paint took the swelling out of the wood. A separate tale type connects the hoopsnake with the motif of the mechanical contrivance mistaken for a person or animal. In a backwoods town in the Missouri Ozarks an old character rode down the street on a high-wheel bicycle. "Here comes the Devil, a-ridin' a hoop snake," cried a little boy. "Yes," called another, seeing the little wheel behind the big one, "an' there's a young hoop snake a-follerin' like a colt."[106]

While Cox omitted the hoopsnake from his bestiary, Brown, Tryon, and Schwartz all acknowledged its claims, which became more obvious as collectors filed their reports. Brown added a new twist, that the only way to avoid the hoopsnake as it approaches is to jump boldly through the hoop, thus confusing the serpent which has rolled past and cannot reverse its momentum. Brown also connected the swollen peavy handle with Paul Bunyan, who cut a thousand cords of wood from the magnified object.[107] Tryon followed this Bunyan bit but added the wrinkle that the only way to outrun a hoopsnake is to climb over a fence and make the snake unhoop to get through.[108] Schwartz liked Randolph's version of the swelling tree whose wood was used for a cowshed that shrunk into a doghouse, and his illustrator Rounds sauced the tale with a drawing of a disconsolate cow and farmer staring at the diminished structure into which a dog was entering.[109]

NINE

The Sea Serpent

THROUGHOUT American history the sea serpent has enjoyed a ubiquitous and tenacious existence. What is remarkable about the Sea Serpent is not what it does but simply that it is seen. No cycle of adventures or special attributes distinguish this reptile, as they do the hoopsnake, save for its size and fearsome appearance. The sighting constitutes the core of the tale, not only in ocean waters but also on the Great Lakes, lesser lakes and inland waterways. Attitudes range from the sincere in the colonial years to the fabulous and hoaxing in later times, but the element of belief has not yet entirely vanished.

A gossipy voyager to America in 1638, John Josselyn, Gent., as he styled himself, related some marvels disclosed to him by settlers greeting him on his arrival, among which was "a Sea *Serpent* or *Snake,* that lay quoiled up like a Cable upon a Rock at *Cape-Ann;* a Boat passing by with *English* aboard, and two *Indians,* they would have shot the *Serpent,* but the Indians disswaded them, saying, that if he were not killed out-right, they would be all in danger of their lives."[110]

This appearance at Cape Ann and the town of Nahant continued to be reported by God-fearing observers, as Obadiah Turner confirms in an entry in his journal in 1641 written in Nahant:

Some being on the great beach gathering of clams and seaweed which had been cast thereon by the mighty storm did spy a most wonderful serpent a short way off from the shore. He was as big round in the thickest part as a wine pipe; and they do affirme that he was fifteen fathoms or more in length. A most wonderful tale. But the witnesses be credible, and it would be of no account to them to tell an untrue tale.

We have likewise heard that at Cape Ann the people have seen a monster like unto this, which did there come out of the sea and coil himself upon the land much to the terror of them that did see him.

And the Indians do say that they have many times seen a wonderful big serpent lying on the water, and reaching from Nahauntus to the great rock which we call Bird's Egg Rock: which is much above belief for it would be nigh upon a mile. The Indians, as said, be given to making the white people stare. But making all discount, I do believe that a wonderful monster in form of a serpent doth visit these waters. And my prayer to God is that it be not the old serpent spoken of in Holy Scripture that tempted our great mother Eve and whose poison hath run down even unto us, so greatly to our discomfort and ruin.[111]

This fine text evinces proper skepticism toward both the white and Indian testimonies and yet comes down on the side of acceptance. Too many worthy eye-witnesses had described the serpent for this Puritan to doubt them, and God's holy writ testified to the existence of such a species.

Nahant on Boston's North Shore long maintained its traditional association with the monster of the deep. In his compilation of New England literary and poetical legends assembled in 1883, Samuel Adams Drake placed "The Sea-Serpent" in his section on "Nahant Legends," with a text illustration, and remarked how the "most exaggerated reports of his length prevailed throughout all the fishing towns of Cape Ann, and up and down the length of the coast."[112] In August 1817, scores of spectators observed the creature in Gloucester Bay. Spurred by the offer of a large reward, vessels were fitted out, nets laid, and the revenue vessel on station ordered to keep a sharp lookout, but to no avail. Drake reprinted a "Sonnet to the Sea-Serpent" by the poet John G. Brainard, which concludes:

But go not to Nahant, lest men should swear
You are a great deal bigger than you are.

In *Jonathan Draws the Long Bow*, I reprint New England news-paper stories of the sea serpent, illustrating the shift from the sober to the ludicrous. In 1719 the Boston *News-Letter* reported a "re-markable Relation" of a "very strange and unusual creature" sighted in Cape Cod, which eluded whalers after a five-hour chase. But by 1769 the *Essex* (Salem) *Gazette* likened British customs col-lectors in New London harbor to "an ill-looking voracious Sea Mon-ster." From the early nineteenth century on, the daily and weekly newspapers presented comic sea-serpent yarns as standard fare. As representative examples I reproduced a wild tall tale from *Jonathan Jaw-Stretcher's Yankee Story All-My-Nack* for 1852, and a mock sighting of an enormous and voracious monster that ate up camp commodities, titled "The Sea Serpent Appears, Seen in Dead Creek by Three Reliable Citizens," from the *Swanton* (Vermont) *Courier* in 1909.[113]

Not only New England but the whole country has reported strange water denizens. Charles M. Skinner devoted eight pages to "Monsters and Sea Serpents" in *Myths and Legends of Our Own Land* (1896) and seven more to "Some Snakes" in *American Myths and Legends* (1903).[114] In his first round-up he mentioned sightings at Cape Ann, 1638; Devil's Lake, Wisconsin, 1892; the Wabash River in Huntington, Indiana; the area of the Twin Lakes in the Berkshire Hills, 1890; Sysladobosis Lake in Maine; Wolf Pond, Pennsylvania, 1897; Silver Lake near Gainesville, New York, 1855; and various Indian monsters in Iowa, Arizona, New York, Oregon, Washington, Wyoming, and other states. In his second round-up he cited serpents from the Chain Lakes, Maine; Cape Cod; Thompson's Lake, Illinois; Devil's Lake, North Dakota, 1896; and Tahoe, California, whose lake serpent he portrayed as a terror six hundred feet long that brushed aside quarter-ton boulders as if they were pebbles. Skinner of course gives no sources, some dates, and little substance for his serpentine meanderings, and his narrative power faltered when confronted by these do-nothing dragons.

By the twentieth century, lake serpents have clearly overtaken sea serpents in folk popularity, although generically they belong to the same class. Charles E. Brown gathered a garland of *Sea Ser-pents* in 1942 in one of his ten-page folklore booklets, but they all were seen in inland waters. The subtitle ran: "Wisconsin Occur-rences of These Weird Water Monsters in the Four Lakes, Rock, Red,

Cedar, Koshkonong, Geneva, Elkhart, Michigan and Other Lakes."
Brown dated the first Wisconsin specimen from 1882 and attributed
the reports of Wisconsin water dragons to mistaken perceptions of
floating logs and overturned boats, the energies of summer resort
promoters, and the fancies of the superstitious and the jocular. University of Wisconsin students in Madison, boaters in Rock Lake, and
fishermen in Red Cedar Lake describe their visions of sea serpents
in newspaper accounts in the 1880s and 1890s that give close details
of their appearances. Bozho in Lake Madison even tickled the feet
of a coed.[115]

In my field trip to the Upper Peninsula of Michigan in 1946, I
spoke with commercial fishermen on Lake Superior who had viewed
a strange creature, like a goose or a loon, that swam faster than
their motor boat and made a wave like an airplane.[116] They obviously believed they had seen something uncanny.

In recent years three folklorists have devoted attention to lake
serpents which made legendary waves in Utah, New York, and Arkansas. Let us glance at their findings.

The Bear Lake Monsters

Sightings of a monster in Bear Lake in Rich County, Utah, first
gained newspaper notice in 1868, and Austin Fife traced the history
of subsequent reports for the next eighty years in an article on "The
Bear Lake Monsters."[117] He asserts the impossibility of relating
"even a small portion of the endless contemporary accounts of the
Bear Lake Monster." Many of these accounts are deadly serious. In
one such story, the Salt Lake *Semi-Weekly Herald* for July 14, 1877,
included an affidavit from one J. H. McNeil, who stated: "It was a
great animal like a crocodile, or alligator, approaching the bank,
but much larger than I have ever heard of one being. It must have
been seventy-five feet long; but the head was not like an alligator's;
it was more like a horse's. When within a few yards of the shore it
made a loud noise and my companion and I fled up the mountain,
where we stayed all night."[118] The Salt Lake paper suspected a hoax
but acknowledged the responsible character of the source. Other
accounts mock the legend, as in this narrative related to Fife in
1946 by a Scout Executive in Cache Valley:

> In the early days in the history of Cache Valley, and especially

in the early days of Bear Lake Valley, there was nothing but a very crude wagon road connecting Bear Lake Valley with Cache Valley, and it was at least a two-day trip to go from Cache Valley to Bear Lake Valley. At that time it was over Mud Flat and down into Round Valley.

There was a certain family in Logan that decided they'd like to go over to Bear Lake and spend a couple of days—there were a couple of families. They hitched up a team on an old light spring wagon and spent the first night half-way through the canyon. The next afternoon about three or four o'clock they arrived at the Lake.

Everybody thought, "Boy, wouldn't a swim be swell!" The beach was quite open and sandy. They drove the team onto the beach and unhitched the horses and tied them to the wagon and gave them some hay—quite a bunch of hay. The two fathers and mothers got into their bathing suits and went down on to the slope of the beach and were just enjoying themselves in a grand way.

All at once there was a great commotion in the water. Big waves were coming in. All at once they noticed the water line was receding down the beach. They couldn't quite understand it. They looked out into the lake and a great monster was coming up—his head was already up. He was as big as a couple of box cars. He was marching up toward shore. He opened his mouth— just imagine, he had a mouth as big as a box car—and he was coming toward them. The water was receding until there wasn't any water near them. They didn't know what to do. They called the kids and started toward the wagon and just as they were about to reach the wagon the monster opened his mouth and was going to take them every one in it, with the wagon and horses, and a little dog began to bark and it distracted his attention, and he looked back and saw his ugly self coming up out of the water like a long train of twenty-five box cars. He saw how ugly he was and he began to cry and the tears were so copious that they washed him back into the lake.[119]

Shades of the catch tale about Oscar the turtle and the piece of ass pinned on John Gutowski by the "Philosopher" of Churubusco! In Fife's material on the Bear Lake monsters we see again two dominant narrative forms displayed: the sober eyewitness sighting and the funmaking jape.

The Serpent of Silver Lake

A serpent in Silver Lake, Wyoming County, in the state of New York attracted widespread attention after first being sighted on July

13, 1855, by four men and two boys from the town of Perry. Harry S. Douglas, history teacher and editor of *Historical Wyoming,* wrote up "The Legend of the Serpent" for a folklore journal, drawing upon newspaper accounts from 1855 to 1860 and the town history of Perry, but he gives no footnoted sources nor any information about Perry and its citizenry. His article indicates the crescendo of interest that developed after the *Perry Times* broke the story on July 18, 1855, and other newspapers, such as the *Buffalo Advertiser* and the *Chicago Times,* recapitulated the details of the original and subsequent sightings. Thousands of curious visitors thronged the hotels and rooming houses of Perry from late July through September, and some entrepreneurs organized the Experiment Company to capture and exhibit the creature. Viewers agreed that the serpent was dark green with yellow spots, a head several feet long, a fierce mouth with sharp fangs and a pointed tongue, and red eyes, the entire reptile reaching some 80 to 100 feet in length. Newspaper reactions varied from credence to ridicule. But the serpent disappeared in the fall of 1855 and was seen no more, in the lake anyway. Two years later, when firemen were battling a fire in the Walker House in Perry, they discovered a contraption of coiled wire and canvas of serpentine dimensions. At length the facts came out that the hotel proprietor, A. B. Walker, with some friends had conceived the idea of manufacturing a serpent in a local tannery to boost summer tourist business and capitalize on an Indian tradition of a lake monster. They anchored their creation at the lake's bottom, and through a mechanism of a bellows on shore, a pipe, rubber tube, ropes, and weights, managed at long distance to inflate, deflate, and maneuver the India rubber reptile before the startled gaze of fishermen and boaters. Several close calls from fishing parties convinced the connivers to secrete the dummy in the hotel attic. Meanwhile, the proprietor and the local editor, who issued special editions with drawings of the serpent, enjoyed the temporary boom in tourism.[120]

The White River Monster

All the vague and loose paraphrasings of serpent and monster sightings make a folklorist squirm with desire to read a proper field inquiry, and fortunately one has newly appeared, dealing with the White River Monster of Jackson County, Arkansas.[121] The investigator, William Harris, a high school teacher interested in the non-Ozark folklore of eastern Arkansas, resided in Newport, the locale of the White River Monster. One Bramlette Bateman first reported the "huge entity" in June, 1937; the Newport Chamber of Commerce picked up the story, and metropolitan Mid-South newspapers gave it full treatment. Harris interviewed Bateman in 1971 and has reconstructed:

> . . . the 1937 scene when the White River Monster turned his [Bateman's] farm into a tourist attraction. A gate was installed at the entrance to the farm, admission was collected, soft drink and snack bar concessions lined the road, a makeshift stage was constructed, bands played, and people danced on the riverbank for several weeks of the Summer of 1937 as tourists, curiosity seekers, newspaper and radio reporters, hawkers, romancers, and local residents . . . came and departed along the banner-lined dirt road from Newport to Bateman Farm.[122]

Interest faded after that year but was rekindled in 1971 by a reporter for the *Newport Independent,* who announced: "Monster returns to Newport after thirty-four year disappearance." A new wave of boosterism now featured "T-shirts illustrating the White River Monster, newspaper drawing contests with prizes, bumper stickers advertising Newport as the home of the White River Monster, and an Arkansas Senate resolution adopting refuge for the monster."[123] Harris conducted twenty-two interviews with Jackson County residents and combed the files of Little Rock, Memphis, and Newport newspapers. His publication of tape transcripts, newspaper bibliography, map of the sightings, and analysis of the data make this a model study of a water-monster legend. Harris's findings eliminate the possibility, accepted by several informants, of an Indian origin and determine the inception of the tradition in 1937. The evidence shows that, in spite of the general indifference of blacks to the monster, a black woman initiated the tale in all seriousness. Bramlette Bateman plays the same true believer role with the White River Monster as did Gale Harris with the Beast of 'Busco. Bateman stated that, while in the company of the black woman who had first seen and been frightened by the creature (but who denied Harris an interview), he too spied it on the river and attempted to shoot it when the sheriff stopped him. For the next two years Bateman continued to see the monster in a deep hole in White River. He declared: "They want to claim it's the Newport's Monster. But it's not the Newport's Monster. It's my Monster." Pressed for details, he likened it to an old Buick, scaly on top, but twice as long and twice as wide.[124]

Other informants discredited the sightings as distorted perceptions of upturned flatbottomed boats, floating garbage, or a big fish or beaver. A retired gas company employee told Harris how he had composed a yarn in 1972 or 1973 to people at the gas company about seeing the monster (pronounced *monuster*):

> Had long, green hair, big old head—looked kind of life a hippopotamus' head except it didn't have no ears. Looked kind of like big old green watermelons weighed about a hundred pounds apiece on each side . . . like's on a toad's head. And his nostrils—you could've throwed a basketball easily into either of one of them. His eyeballs was about the size of a number two washtub, and he turned one of the eyeballs and looked right at us—old green eye—turned that old green eye and looked right straight at us. Well, when he seen us, he turned in that river so fast that he splashed water plumb over that bank which was about four foot high.[125]

The listeners to this account wrote it up in a letter to the editor who printed it as a truthful report. Harris concludes that the legend of the monster, propelled by both believers and hoaxers and stimulated by the interplay of oral and media stories, will continue for some time.[126]

TEN

Bigfoot

A giant apelike monster has effected a late entry into the American bestiary but appears to be making up for lost time with the intensity of the stir he has created. The populace and the media have dubbed him Bigfoot, in recognition of the size of his footprints, which range in length from eight to twenty inches and in width to three times that of a human foot. Across the Canadian border in the Northwest this creature is called Sasquatch and blends with Indian traditions, while his cousin in the Himalayas is known as Yeti or the Abominable Snowman. In 1972, one Bigfoot biographer, John Napier, curator of primate collections in the Smithsonian Institution, wrote that the reports about Bigfoot lacked a narrative element and concentrated on sightings, either of the footprints or of the six to nine foot being itself.[127] These sightings in the United States commenced in northern California in the 1920s and spread to Oregon and Washington, with 1969 a peak year. Reactions vary from the true believers to the scoffers.

The most sensational episode in the Bigfoot business developed in Minnesota with the disclosure in 1968 of a hominoid creature frozen in a block of ice kept in a coffin on a northern farm. Two zoologists, a Belgian, Bernard Heuvelmans, and an American, Ivan T. Sanderson, examined the "Iceman," as he was dubbed and pronounced him authentic. Heuvelmans formally classified him *Homo pongoides*. Its

71

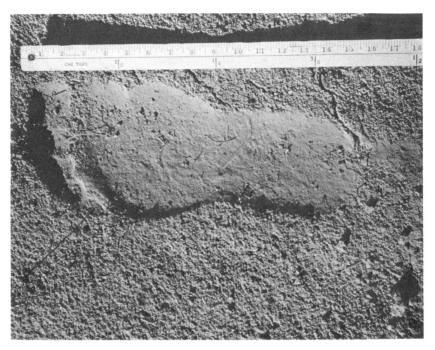

Sasquatch track, 15 inches long, found on Blue Creek Mountain, California, 1967.

captor, Frank D. Hansen, a farmer, claimed that he had found the creature floating in the Sea of Okhotsk off eastern Siberia. The Smithsonian Institution with the approval of its Secretary, S. Dillon Ripley, agreed to investigate the Minnesota Iceman, only to learn that a multi-millionaire movie magnate living in Hollywood, interested in rarities, owned the creature and had withdrawn it from the possession of Hansen, who planned to exhibit a model to the public. Next, several commercial organizations asserted that they had fabricated the Iceman out of latex rubber and human hair. J. Edgar Hoover and the F.B.I. declined to become involved, and the Smithsonian withdrew its interest. Hansen now displayed "The Near-Man, the Siberskoye Creature, Investigated by the F.B.I." at carnivals for thirty-five cents admission. Public interest was maintained by a newspaper revelation on June 30, 1969, "I was raped by the Abominable Snowman," from a young woman who stated that she had shot the nearly twelve-foot man-thing while hunting near

Bemidiji, Minnesota. Next the papers carried an elaborate reconstruction of the affair by Frank Hansen telling how he had shot and killed the strange hairy creature in northern Minnesota in 1960 while he was still in the Air Force and refrigerated the creature for seven years, fearing no one would credit his story.[128]

Three sleuths have filmed Bigfoot. One in California in 1957 took 15,000 feet of color film, showing a Bigfoot picking up fifty-gallon drums of grease and throwing them 150 feet. A second in Colville, Washington, in 1969 filmed seventy feet of a crippled Bigfoot nine feet high and weighing 800 pounds. But by far the most convincing was the sequence shot by Roger Patterson in Bluff Creek Valley in northern California in 1967. Patterson's 16 mm. film reveals a female Bigfoot walking along a dried-up stream-bed, then turning her back to the camera and disappearing into the forest. Napier examined the film repeatedly and reproduces a frame in his book.[129] He published the statement that he could see nothing in the film to prove it a hoax, but he also admitted that "the scientific evidence taken collectively points to a hoax of some kind."[130]

Besides the rash of sightings in the Pacific Northwest, viewers have spotted Bigfoot between 1964 and 1970 in fourteen states in the Midwest, Midsouth, and as far east as Pennsylvania and Georgia. Hence Napier concludes that it is impossible "to say that it does not exist."[131] The composite picture that emerges is of an upright-walking humanlike being covered with reddish-brown hair, with head hair falling half a dozen inches over the forehead, broad and deep shoulders, a short neck resembling that of a football player, and an apelike face with sloping forehead and lipless mouth.[132]

In *Bigfoot, America's Abominable Snowman* (published in 1975), Elwood D. Baumann, who had previously written *The Loch Ness Monster*, presented a series of thirty-eight narrative vignettes of sightings of the man-ape. A frontispiece shows a painting, based on a blowup of a frame in Patterson's film, of a female Bigfoot, covered with hair all over her body and down over her conical head to her eyes. The flat nose, thin lips and dull eyes of a hulking creature walking warily through the woods lead the viewers to wonder whether Bigfoot is indeed humanoid or anthropoid. Baumann, a onetime overseas school teacher and energetic traveler, is a believer and a crusader. He introduces other crusaders, one being Jim McClarin, who dropped out of Humboldt State College to devote his life

Rene Dahinden displaying 14½-inch sasquatch track cast and Roger Patterson with 17 x   7½-inch cast. Both found at Bluff Creek, California, 1964 and 1967 respectively.

to capturing Bigfoot. McClarin carved the eight-foot statue of Bigfoot which greets visitors to Willow Creek, the center of Bigfoot spottings in northern California.

Anyone who captures, exhibits, or kills Bigfoot faces serious legal problems, McClarin learned. The California Fish and Game Code docs not provide for the capture of Bigfoot, should he prove to be an animal. Were Bigfoot killed, and proved to be a human, his killer would be prosecuted for murder under the California Penal Code. Or if he were not killed but displayed for profit, the showman would still face a death rap, under California's Little Lindbergh Law. An editorial in the *Humboldt Standard* proposed making Bigfoot an honorary citizen of California, in recognition of all he had done for tourism.[133]

Another consecrated Bigfoot hunter, Ron Olson, of Eugene, Oregon, constructed a huge cage baited with assorted goodies to trap the big fellow. If his curiosity should lead Bigfoot to the food, an electronically controlled door would slam shut behind him. "I know that the trap works because I've already caught two bears and an Indian," Olson cracked, in a joke not funny in the current sensitivities.[134] The mixture of the deadly serious testimony and the spoofing letter, cartoon, and gag marks the Bigfoot mania. Believer Baumann omits all mentions of the Minnesota hoax creature that fooled Ivan Sanderson. He does recognize that:

> Bigfoot is rapidly becoming big business in little Willow Creek, population one thousand, in the heart of the Douglas fir country. Tourists eagerly buy Bigfoot postcards and "lifelike" statuettes of the hairy giant. There's a Bigfoot Dance Club, and something is always going on at Bigfoot Golf and Country Club. Each Labor Day weekend, a celebration is held in honor of Bigfoot.
> Bigfoot Daze . . . begins with a Bigfoot breakfast. The crowning of the Bigfoot queen follows. . . .
> The three-day program includes a whiskering contest in which bearded men are judged, go-cart races, a barbecue followed by a Bigfoot Dance, a frog-jumping contest, and a host of other events.[135]

Napier's book further notes that footprints are emblazoned on the Willow Creek sidewalks and that every local tourist shop sells Bigfoot ashtrays and Bigfoot rings. Unlike the solemn scientific air that cloaks the quest for the Loch Ness monster, Bigfoot has taken on an American dimension of boosterism and horseplay. Napier observes with distaste, "Bigfoot in some quarters of North America has become Big Business, a commodity to be exploited to the full. It can no longer be considered simply as a natural phenomenon that can be studied with the techniques of a naturalist; the enterpreneurs have moved in and folklore has become fakelore."[136]

What the bullfrogs mean to Windham, the turtle to Churubusco, and the jackalope to Douglas, Bigfoot has become to Willow Creek: a special and profitable property that distinguishes one small American town from all its counterparts.

PART *ii*

Munchausens

American folklore has produced a special kind of folk hero, one who acquires local renown for spinning tall tales about his own feats and in effect creates his own legend which other storytellers perpetuate. The folklorists who have collected the tale-cycles refer to their heroes as Munchausens, after a German cavalry officer, Karl Friedrich Hieronymus, Baron von Münchhausen (1720–1797), who related wondrous accounts to boon companions about his adventures soldiering, traveling, and hunting. *Baron Munchausen's Narrative of his Marvellous Travels and Campaigns in Russia* appeared in Oxford in 1786 in a translation from a German periodical by a talented scoundrel named Rudolf Erich Raspe.[1] Münchhausen drew his tales from ongoing oral tradition, and some have crossed the ocean and entered the repertoires of his American counterparts.

Eight American Munchausens whose biographies and tale-cycles are now on record (some in considerable detail, others sketchily) are here presented. All lived in the latter decades of the nineteenth century and some into the twentieth. The earliest birth date of the eight is 1796, and the latest death date is 1950. The earliest death date is 1881, and the latest birth date is 1878. All were alive in 1880. The eight were all outdoorsmen. Five were basically farmers: Oregon Smith, John Darling, Len Henry, Jones Tracy, and Daniel Stamps. Jim Bridger was a trapper and guide. Hathaway Jones

77

carried the mail by mule across mountain passes. Gib Morgan drilled for oil. All hunted and fished. They lived in the northern tier of states from Maine to Oregon (although I am sure their fellows exist in the South). Each possessed the characteristics necessary to the creation of a Munchausen folk hero, namely the skill at storytelling and a colorful personality, somewhat comic or eccentric, that would make each raconteur a subject as well as a reciter of anecdotes. The Munchausens spun windies about their exploits of hunting, fishing, shooting, and lifting, and lesser storytellers told about their oddities, trickery, or ability to draw the long bow. Two cycles of tales thus keep alive the legend of the fabulists: stories about their actual behavior and retellings by others of their favorite tall tales.

While certain standard tale types, such as "The Wonderful Hunt" or "Sinking into Rock under a Heavy Weight," unite the repertoires of the various Munchausens, each boasts an individual strain. Jim Bridger yarns about the wonders of Yellowstone; Oregon Smith about the wonders of Oregon and the properties of his sassafras oil; Gib Morgan about his fabulous strikes while drilling for oil; Len Henry about his ability as roper and rider; Hathaway Jones about his conquests of blizzards and mountain slides; Jones Tracy about his skill as a deer hunter; Dan'l Stamps about weather extremes in Arkansas and Iowa; John Darling about surprises on his farm. Their collective fantasies sketch a gallery of outdoor supermen with a comic twist.

Secondary Munchausens

Careful collectors of tall tale hero cycles agree on the point that the primary Munchausen personality stands out among a stellar circle of storytellers. Indeed were there no other raconteurs in the vicinity, the legends of these exaggerating heroes would have ended with their deaths. A distinction needs to be made between the storyteller who glorifies himself and the storyteller who is content to repeat the glories attached to the deceased fabulist. Some expert tall tale tellers, like Bill Greenfield of New York State, who shared some of John Darling's repertoire, reach only a certain level of attention, perhaps because others did not develop his legend.[2]

Conscientious folklorists acknowledge their debts to the storytelling successors of their Munchausens. William H. Jansen discussed carefully the narrative techniques of Abe Smith's emulators, particularly Frank Newlin, who as a young man in Chrisman ran a grocery store where Lying Abe liked to loaf and spin his yarns. After Smith's death Newlin continued to relate tales associated with Abe, even to mimicking his speech and burlesquing his walk. Newlin's artistry was thus described by an observer: "Frank Newlin had Old Abe down. He could do Old Abe so's you'd swear it was Abe himself." This speaker, Guy Scott, after Newlin's death in turn became the most noted storyteller in Chrisman, and would relate Abe's stories with circumstantial details and a pixie humor that greatly impressed Jansen. For sixty years the town of Chrisman enjoyed the presence of a skilled narrator, from Smith to Newlin to Scott, as well as lesser lights, who maintained the cycle of Lying Abe.[3]

Historian Stephen Dow Beckham, the biographer of Hathaway Jones, mentions other Munchausens of the Rogue River country who retold Hathaway's tales and also produced their own. Beckham singled out pioneer John Fitzhugh, who died in 1903, a ballad singer as well as a fabulist, and reprinted two of his personal yarns from a local paper; and John Fry, who mined in the area, and lived forty-three years longer than Fitzhugh. Thus the Munchausen tradition continued in the Rogue River country for nearly a century, from the time Fitzhugh entered the region in 1855. An intermediate collector, Arthur Dorn, who supplied Beckham with many Hathaway Jones yarns, obtained his narratives not only from Hathaway Jones himself (as well as John Fry) but from five other Rogue River residents: a hotel proprietor, three trappers and guides, and the owner of a pie shop. Sitting on a porch or a cabin doorstep, they heard Hathaway relate his sagas as he traveled along his mail route.[4]

In *Jones Tracy, Tall-Tale Hero from Mount Desert Island,* folklorist C. Richard K. Lunt offered a comparison between the narrative style of the previous generation of Mount Desert Island storytellers, exemplified by Tracy, and the current generation, from whom Lunt collected. For this purpose he chose Chauncy Somes, stone cutter and shipwright, sixty in 1963, whose reputation as yarnspinner had led to his being invited to narrate at the Somesville Bi-Centennial celebration two years before. A clear contrast emerged between the deliveries of Tracy and Somes, both of whom excelled in tale-telling in the same area forty years apart, and each of whom fairly repre-

sented the master narrators of his generation. Tracy indulged in
leisurely, drawn out narrations furnished with realistic dialogue
and settings. Chauncy pared the same stories to their cores, and
emphasized the punchline ending. In Somes's condensations the tall
tale, dependent on its naturalistic depiction before its final leap into
the impossible, contracts into the joke. In his day Jones Tracy could
spin out his chronicle in the deer hunter's cabin or the dance hall or
other social gathering places. By Chauncy Somes's time loafing and
idling had gone out as pastimes, and stories are told on the run, to
match the speeded-up tempo of life. As Lunt well puts it, reposeful
leisure has given way to active leisure. Somes keeps alive Tracy's
tall tales, but at the expense of the heroics of legend. The tall-tale
hero becomes a figure of fun. This change in the rhythms of American lifestyle may explain why our Munchausens all belong to a
bygone era.

ONE

Jim Bridger

(1804–1881)

J IM Bridger gained fame as mountain man, fur trader, scout, guide, and Indian fighter. Friend and mentor of Kit Carson, whom he supposedly introduced to General John C. Fremont, Bridger was known to all the leading entrepreneurs of the West. Bernard DeVoto sums up Bridger's career when he states, "He had survived the far West, through its entire existence, by virtue of a skill never surpassed on this continent. . . . He was the West."[5] As early as 1849 an army officer, in an expedition guided by Jim, told friends: "that Bridger was the leading man then in the mountains; his influence with the Indians was greater than any other man's sway; and his capabilities as a guide were unsurpassed."[6]

Stories about Bridger's exploits and eccentricities regaled officers and soldiers, emigrants and fellow mountain men, and all who passed through the West in the mid-nineteenth century decades, save perhaps the Mormons resentful of his intrusion. In these narratives he emerged as a frontier hero, as a character, and as a storyteller. A captain in the United States Cavalry, James Lee Humfreville, who called Old Jim "the most efficient guide, mountaineer, plainsman, trapper and Indian fighter that ever lived in the Far West,"[7] wrote about Bridger in all three roles.

Bridger's fame transcended campfire circles and was further propelled by popular print writings. Ned Buntline, king of the dime

Jim Bridger

novelists exploiting the Far West, interviewed the old guide at his
Missouri farm in 1860 and accompanied him on a scouting trip
across the plains. According to General Grenville M. Dodge, Buntline on returning east began publishing Jim Bridger stories once a
week, which Jim's comrades read to him. "Buntline made Bridger
famous, and carried him through more hairbreadth escapes than
any man ever had."[8] Buntline also publicized the mountaineer as a
romancer, the author of "old Jim Bridger's Lies."

After Jim's death another celebrated writer of western adventure,
Emerson Hough, put Bridger in his novel *The Covered Wagon*
(1922), and portrayed him as a heavy drinker, womanizer, and dis-
torter of facts. Incensed, Bridger's heirs brought suit against the

mountain man John Smith, and in disgust at the idea of his friend trying to bamboozle him, Bridger cried out, "Hell, Bill, you can't fool me! That's old John Smith." In a related tale, Bridger meets the President in Washington, turns to the congressman who had introduced him and says, "Looks jest like any other man, don't he?"[15]

On his first visit to St. Louis, a friend came across Bridger sitting disconsolately on a drygoods box in a narrow street. When asked what he was doing there all alone, Bridger replied, "I've been settin' in this infernal cañon ever sence mornin', waitin' for some one to come along an' invite me to take a drink. Hundreds of fellers has passed both ways, but none of 'em has opened his head. I never seen sich a unsociable crowd."[16] In a variant Jim responds to a mountaineer friend, "I'm trying to find my way out of these ____cañons," and adds morosely, "This is the meanest camp I ever struck in my life. I have met more'n a thousand men in the last hour, and nary one of 'em has asked me to come to his lodge and have something to eat."[17]

Had he never spun a yarn, Bridger would still have left his mark as a mountain man with legendary skills. Yet posterity remembers him as a teller rather than a subject of marvelous yarns. His tall tales of Yellowstone Park drew all the more attention because they issued from a celebrated guide. At first Bridger endeavored to report the true wonders he beheld and met with ridicule. The historian of the fur trade and Yellowstone National Park, Hiram M. Chittenden, reports that Bridger first visited Yellowstone in 1830 and revisited it frequently thereafter, but when an editor of a major western newspaper prepared an article on Jim's account of the marvels at Yellowstone, a supposed acquaintance of Bridger told the journalist "he would be laughed out of town if he printed any of 'old Jim Bridger's lies.' "[18] Thirty years later, in 1879, the editor apologized publicly to Bridger for doubting his reports. The historian of the first official exploring party to Yellowstone Park, Nathaniel P. Langford, who met Bridger in Montana in 1866 and heard Jim's account of a hot column of water sixty feet high spouting from the earth, published articles in *Scribner's* in 1871 about the park and received the same kind of disbelief accorded to the guide.[19] Yellowstone's wonders were hard to believe, and Jim exposed himself to ridicule with his serious explanation for the hot current found at the bottom of Firehole River. He described an ice-cold spring flowing down a mountain slope with such velocity that it was boiling hot when it reached the bottom. Langford states that he frequently heard Bridger repeat this marvel of nature and suggest that the friction of water rubbing over the rock on its downward descent produced the heat. Only close to the rock, Jim declared, was the water hot. Langford himself writes that in fording Firehole River in 1870 he crossed barefooted on a smooth rock surface covering the stream's bottom and felt a warmth underfoot as he stood on an incrustation formed over a hot spring beneath the bed of the stream. He exclaimed, "Here is the river which Bridger said was *hot at the bottom.*"[20]

So the old man of the mountains initially pictured Yellowstone truthfully in all its glories. He related to Western explorers scenes of a great cold lake sixty miles long, spouting geysers, thundering waterfalls, a perpendicular canyon, springs so hot meat could be cooked in them, terraces and pools that provide delightful baths, an acid spring, and a cave from which Indians obtained vermilion paint.[21] The Westerners listened, shook their heads, and winked to one another.

Smarting from these rejections and scoffs, Jim turned the tables on his skeptics by deliberately inflating the accounts of these natural wonders. The teller of remarkable true tales shifts gears to become a teller of straightfaced tall tales. Western chroniclers have noted Jim's oral style and storytelling mannerisms. In their annual rendezvous and winter camps, the mountain men would indulge in reminiscences of bear hunts, Indian fights, blizzards and other hair-raising adventures, and Bridger easily acquired the tradition of oral narrating. According to Humfreville, he possessed a quick and vivid imagination and could reel off story after story with astonishing spontaneity and grave mien. In the role of storyteller, he assumed a "peculiar drawling tone," to emphasize his awe-inspiring points. Commanding in appearance, over six feet tall, spare and straight in his younger years, (though hunched over in later life as the result of Indian arrows piercing his body), agile, rawboned, with clean features, gray eyes, abundant brown hair, and mild manners, Jim impressed the immigrants, visitors, and soldiers who questioned him about the West.[22]

A number of these Westerners saw fit to report Bridger's tales and sayings with what appears to be reasonable accuracy, down to the reproduction of Jim's dialogue and expressions. In 1925 one of Jim's biographers, J. Cecil Alter, rounded up all these memoirs and explorers' journals. In a chapter titled "The Beginning of Bridger's Stories," he quoted trappers' tall tales recorded in the journal of Captain W. F. Raynolds, who explored the Yellowstone River and its tributaries in 1859 and 1860. Raynolds set down reports of a petrified forest, a diamond mountain, and a river hot at the bottom. In a later chapter, "The Evolution of Bridger's Stories," Alter added to his stockpile of Bridger's yarns. Writing about Yellowstone National Park in 1895, Hiram M. Chittenden incorporated Jim's vignettes of a petrified mountain, a glass mountain, and a mountain that produced a slow echo. General Nelson A. Miles, publishing his *Personal Recollections* in 1896, related Jim's account of sighting petrified trees, birds, and songs. The following year in *The Old Sante Fe Trail* Colonel Henry Inman recounted Jim's claim to having pickled buffalo in Great Salt Lake. In 1903 J. Lee Humfreville, recalling his *Twenty Years Among Our Hostile Indians,* picked up Bridger's tales about a crystal mountain and the time "the Injun killed me."

In assembling these extravagant tales, Alter recognized their traditional character and used a mouth-filling term, kabajolism (derived from Elbert Hubbard), to denote the folk process of ascribing sayings or writings to persons not responsible for them. Kabajolism was thus the opposite of plagiarism, and most of Bridger's stories, opined Alter, were "pure kabajolisms," planted by a kabajolist who wished to discredit someone without taking the blame himself. Thus Alter considered the anecdotes about Bridger's addiction to drink to be kabajolism,[23] and those making out the mountain man to be an inveterate liar, or a gullible naif, as belonging to "a large school of fish stories which have been kabajolized on a helpless Bridger."[24]

To recapitulate: the documentary evidence discloses a threefold role of Jim Bridger in American legendry: the frontier Indian fighter, the eccentric character, and the Munchausen storyteller. Tales about Jim in his first two guises contributed to the expansion of his Munchausen persona, and, as various chroniclers remarked, the wondrous tales circulating about Yellowstone and the Far West all gravitated to Bridger. Some tales that appeared to be Jim's own inventions belong to a body of traditional whoppers shared by the mountain men and occasionally dating back to earlier frontiers. An example of a formulaic colloquy with a long history can be seen in Jim's offhand observations to tourists and immigrants who pestered him at Fort Bridger about the mineral and vegetable wealth of the western lands. In this exchange he arouses their cupidity with an extravaganza about a gold mine not far from the Overland road:

> "Why, the gold's so plentiful," said Bridger, "that all that's nec-
> essary to secure it is to jest pick it up. Great nuggets of the purest
> gold are scattered all over the ground. There's no diggin' to be
> done, or rock-crushin' machines an' siftin' required. You orter to
> step over and fill your pockets; you'll find it mighty useful on
> your journey. Anybody who's in want of gold need only go there
> an' load himself."
> "Do you mean to say that it is free to anybody?"
> "Free as the air we breathe," said Bridger.
> "How can we get there?" one of the listening crowd ventured
> to inquire.
> "*Hire a buggy*—easiest thing in the world," answered
> Bridger.[25]

The earliest dream about the New World, that its streets were paved with gold, resurfaces in this dialogue. In our day we have seen a new frenzy for gold pushing its market value over eight hundred dollars an ounce. The California and later the Alaskan gold rushes epitomize in our history Americans' fever for the yellow metal. In this little scene Jim—or his kabajolizer—attaches the golden myth to another hallowed indigenous tradition, the gull of the innocent, be he Eastern dude, English traveler, or pesky Yankee, by the solemn-faced native. The dialogue between the Arkansas Traveler and his visitor embodies this formula in a classic state-ment. In Thomas Bangs Thorpe's *The Big Bear of Arkansas*, Jim Doggett regales the steamboat crowd, and in particular a wide-eyed Englishman, with the wonders of Arkansas. A snapper in the pres-ent snatch of dialogue derives from the fact that no buggy could be procured within six hundred miles of Fort Bridger.

On one occasion General Gatlin, commander of Fort Gibson in the Cherokee Nation, asked Bridger if he had ever seen the great can-yon of the Colorado River:

> "Yes, sir," replied the mountaineer, "I have, many a time.
> There's where the oranges and lemons bear all the time, and the
> only place I was ever at where the moon's always full!"[26]

Here is America, the land of milk and honey, exemplified in a thousand scattered tall tales of giant fruits and fast-growing vegetables.[27] Another Munchausen, Oregon Smith, would tell about turnips in Oregon as large as pumpkins.[28]

A further example of Bridger's response to an inquisitor concerns the awesome landscape:

> At one time when in camp near "Pumpkin Butte," a well-known landmark near Fort Laramie, rising a thousand feet or more above the surrounding plain, a young 'attache' of the party approached Mr. Bridger, and in a rather patronizing manner said: "Mr. Bridger, they tell me that you have lived a long time on these plains and in the mountains."
>
> Mr. Bridger, pointing toward "Pumpkin Butte," replied: "Young man, you see that butte over there! Well, that mountain was a *hole in the ground* when I came here."[29]

Stories of phenomenal size and growth commenced with the first travelers' tales about America and gradually stretched into long bows. A current joke along this line reports a conversation between a New Yorker and a foreign tourist who expressed amazement at the sight of the Empire State Building and asked how long it had taken to erect that skyscraper. "I can't say," replied the New Yorker, "it wasn't there yesterday." The myth of American fecundity is here extended from natural to manmade phenomena. Bridger's tall tales about the West fit into the theme of Schlaraffenland, the earthly paradise where roast pigs waddle around with knives and forks stuck in their sides.[30]

Some half dozen of Bridger's accounts of nature's wonders in the fabled West acquired special distinction and enhanced his legend. Unlike ubiquitous tall tales about skillful marksmanship and fast-growing vegetables, these narrations dealt with the landscape, a landscape such as only the western country could produce.

The Petrified Forest

Jim Bridger's most celebrated tale dealt with a petrified mountain. Chittenden gave this verson in 1895:

> According to his [Bridger's] account there exists in the Park country a mountain which was once cursed by a great medicine man of the Crow nation. Every thing upon the mountain at the time of this dire event became instantly petrified and has remained so ever

since. All forms of life are standing about in stone where they were suddenly caught by the petrifying influences, even as the inhabitants of ancient Pompeii were surprised by the ashes of Vesuvius. Sage brush, grass, prairie fowl, antelope, elk, and bears may there be seen as perfect as in actual life. Even flowers are blooming in colors of crystal, and birds soar with wings spread in motionless flight, while the air floats with music and perfumes siliceous, and the sun and the moon shine with petrified light![31]

A narrative episode attached to the Petrified Mountain appears to be too fanciful even for Bridger, and, in the eyes of Chittenden (as quoted by Alter) is probably the product of a later kabajolizer:

According to this anonymous authority, Bridger, one evening after a long day's ride, was approaching a familiar camping place in this region of petrifications but from a direction not before taken. Quite unexpectedly he came upon a narrow, deep, precipitous chasm which completely blocked his way. Exhausted as both he and his horse were with their long march, he was completely disheartened at this obstacle, to pass which, might cause him several hours of strenuous exertion and carry him far into the night.

Riding up to the brink to reconnoiter he found that he could not stop his horse, which kept moving right along as if by its own momentum, out over the edge of the precipice, straight on at a steady gait and on a level line, as if supported by an invisible bridge. Almost before he realized it he was safe on the other side, and in his desired camp. His utter amazement at this miracle soon abated when he remembered the strange character of the country he was in, and he concluded that this chasm was simply a place where the attraction of gravitation was petrified.[32]

Another report of petrification is attributed to Bridger by General Nelson Miles:

"The story is told that on some such (story-telling) occasion, one night after supper, a comrade who in his travels and explorations had gone as far south as the Zuni village, New Mexico, and had discovered the famous petrified forest of Arizona, inquired of Bridger:

"Jim, were you ever down to Zuni?"

"No, thar ain't any beaver down thar."

"But Jim, there are some things in this world besides beaver. I was down there last winter and saw great trees with limbs and bark and all turned into stone."

" 'O', returned Jim, "that's peetrifaction. Come with me to the

> Yellowstone next summer, and I'll show you petrified trees a grow-
> ing, with petrified birds on 'em a-singing peetrified songs.' "[33]

Miles explains the naturalistic basis of this wonder in Jim's having seen trees covered with the hot water ejected by the geysers and
carried several hundred feet in the air. The carbonate of lime and
geyserite in the water gave the appearance of a crystal formation
on the rear side of the trees, while living Branches grew on the far
side. Captain W. F. Raynolds, who led an expedition to Yellowstone
in 1859–60, commented on "Munchausen tales" told in camp by the
mountain men concerning petrification and fossils found throughout
the western country:

> It was claimed that in some locality (I was not able to fix it defi-
> nitely) a large tract of sage is perfectly petrified, with all the leaves
> and branches in perfect condition, the general appearance of the
> plain not being unlike that of the rest of the country, but all is
> stone, while the rabbits, sage hens, and other animals usually
> found in such localities are still there, perfectly petrified, and as
> natural as when they were living; and more wonderful still, these
> petrified bushes bear the most wonderful fruit—diamonds, rubies,
> sapphires, emeralds, etc., as large as black walnuts, are found in
> abundance. 'I tell you, sir,' said one narrator, 'it is true, for I gath-
> ered a quart myself, and sent them down the country.'
> Another story runs in this wise: A party of whites were once
> pursued by Indians so closely that they were forced to hide during
> the day, and could only travel at night. In this they were greatly
> aided by the brilliancy of a large diamond in the face of a neigh-
> boring mountain by the light of which they travelled for three
> consecutive nights.[34]

In these last versions the petrified mountain has given way to a
petrified forest, thus harking back to older traditions which speak
of a forest. In 1823 one Westerner, James Clyman, confided to his
diary the following entry on the subject:

> A mountaineer named Harris [Moses "Black" Harris] being in
> St. Louis some years after [seeing the petrified trees] undertook to
> describe some of the strange things seen in the mountains, spoke
> of this petrified grove, in a restaurant, where a caterer for one of
> the dailies was present; and the next morning his exaggerated
> statement came out saying a petrified forest was lately discovered
> where the tree branches, leaves and all, were perfect, and the small

birds sitting on them, with their mouths open, singing at the time of their transformation to stone.[35]

The description of a "petrified forest" by a mountain trapper named Black Harris appears in 1849 in George Frederick Ruxton's *Life in the Far West*. Harris has come down from the mountains and is relating to a lady in St. Louis, in thick mountain man dialect, his perception of this wondrous tableau. In Ruxton's semi-fictional narrative, another mountain man retells Black Harris's wonder, an indication of how the yarn was being passed around:

> "Surely Black Harris was thar; and the darndest liar was Black Harris—for lies tumbled out of his mouth like boudins out of a bufler's stomach. He was the child as saw the putrefied forest in the Black Hills. Black Harris come in from Laramie; he'd been trapping three year an' more on Platte and the 'other side'; and, when he got into Liberty, he fixed himself right off like a Saint Louiy dandy. Well, he sat to dinner one day in the tavern, and a lady says to him:—
>
> " 'Well, Mister Harris, I hear you're a great travler.'
>
> " 'Travler, marm,' says Black Harris, 'this niggur's no travler; I ar' a trapper, marm, a mountain-man, wagh!'
>
> " 'Well, Mister Harris, trappers are great travlers, and you goes over a sight of ground in your perishinations, I'll be bound to say.'
>
> " 'A sight, marm, this coon's gone over, if that's the way your 'stick floats.'* I've trapped beaver on Platte and Arkansa, and away up on Missoura and Yaller Stone; I've trapped on Columbia, on Lewis Fork, and Green River; I've trapped, marm, on Grand River and the Heely (Gila). I've fout the 'Blackfoot' (and d——d bad Injuns they ar); I've 'raised the hair'† of more *than one* Apach, and made a Rapaho 'come' afore now; I've trapped in heav'n, in airth, and h—; and scalp my old head, marm, but I've seen a putrefied forest.'
>
> " 'La, Mister Harris, a what?'
>
> " 'A putrefied forest, marm, as sure as my rifle's got hind-sights, and *she* shoots center. I was out on the Black Hills, Bill Sublette knows the time—the year it rained fire—and everybody knows when that was. If thar wasn't cold doins about that time, this child wouldn't say so. The snow was about fifty foot deep, and the bufler

---

*Meaning—if that's what you mean. The "stick" is tied to the beaver trap by a string; and, floating on the water, points out its position, should a beaver have carried it away.
† Scalped.

lay dead on the ground like bees after a beein'; not whar we was tho', for *thar* was no bufler, and no meat, and me and my band had been livin' on our mocassins (leastwise the parflesh*) for six weeks; and poor doins that feedin' is, marm, as you'll never know. One day we crossed a 'cañon' and over a 'divide,' and got into a peraira, whar was green grass, and green trees, and green leaves on the trees, and birds singing in the green leaves, and this in Febrary, wagh! Our animals was like to die when they see the green grass, and we all sung out, 'hurraw for summer doins.'

" 'Hyar goes for meat,' says I, and I jest ups old Ginger at one of them singing birds, and down come the crittur elegant; its darned head spinning away from the body, but never stops singing, and when I takes up the meat, I finds it stone, wagh! 'Hyar's damp powder and no fire to dry it,' I says, quite skeared.

" 'Fire be dogged,' says old Rube. 'Hyar's a hos as'll make fire come;' and with that he takes his axe and lets drive at a cotton wood. Schr-u-k—goes the axe agin the tree, and out comes a bit of the blade as big as my hand. We looks at the animals, and thar they stood shaking over the grass, which I'm dog-gone if it wasn't stone, too. Young Sublette comes up, and he'd been clerking down to the fort on Platte, so he know'd something. He looks and looks, and scrapes the trees with his butcher knife, and snaps the grass like pipe stems, and breaks the leaves a-snappin' like Californy shells.'

" 'What's all this, boy?' I asks.

" 'Putrefactions,' says he, looking smart; 'putrefactions, or I'm a niggur.'

" 'La, Mister Harris,' says the lady, 'putrefactions! why, did the leaves and the trees and the grass smell badly?'

" 'Smell badly, marm!' says Black Harris; 'would a skunk stink if he was froze to stone? No, marm, this child didn't know what pu-trefaction was, and young Sublette's varsion wouldn't 'shine' no-how, so I chips a piece out of a tree and puts it in my trap-sack, and carries it in safe to Laramie. Well, old Captain Stewart, (a clever man was that, though he was an Englishman,) he comes along next spring, and a Dutch doctor chap was along too. I shows him the piece I chipped out of the tree, and he called it a putrefaction too; and so, marm, if that wasn't a putrefied peraira, what was it? For this hos doesn't know, and *he* knows 'fat cow' from 'poor bull,' anyhow.'[36]

Now Bridger's reference to the petrified birds singing songs takes on a larger context and appears not as an idle aside but as a splinter

* Soles made of buffalo hide.

of a well established traditional narrative, traceable back to 1823 and attached originally to another mountain man. Again we find the Arkansas Traveler formula, with a sagacious *indigène* impressing the outsider by reciting a series of marvels. The scene contains a frontier boast, in which the self-proclaimed trapper and mountain man sets forth his exploits and caps them with the grandest claim of all, the sight of a "putrified" forest. There follows a series of peripheral tall tales about the rigors of the climate to set the stage. The reference to William L. Sublette, a member and subsequently one of the leaders of the first trapping party of the Rocky Mountain Fur Company that left St. Louis on April 15, 1822 (and included Bridger and Moses Harris), gives us a historical anchorage. Suddenly the green forest looms, and, like Davy Crockett of the almanacs (contemporary with, and in the vein of, Ruxton's account), who referred to his rifle as old Betsy, Harris lets fly with old Ginger. But these are no ordinary birds, and they prove to be stone. Sublette and a Captain Stewart (Alter mentions an "adventurer" Captain Stuart who had come from Fort Laramie to join Sublette at a mountain man rendezvous)[37] support the finding.

Moses Harris, then, first promulgated, so far as we know, the yarn of the petrified grove. In Alter's biography of Bridger, Harris appears as a shadowy figure who accompanies Sublette in 1825 from the winter Salt Lake rendezvous to St. Louis and turns up as scout, trapper leader, and possibly a major in later references.[38] He was said to be one of the party that first navigated the Great Salt Lake. Only once in these scant mentions does Harris assume any personality. Sent to reconnoiter unknown terrain northwest of Yellowstone Park, the scout ascended a high peak, and returned saying he "saw the city of St. Louis and one fellow taking a drink."[39]

Black Harris comes to life in a sketch provided by the historian Charles L. Camp. Born in South Carolina, Harris first became known in Western annals as a member of the Ashley-Henry party of 1822. For years he carried expresses for the fur company from the western side of the Rocky Mountains to Fort Laramie, riding alone all night and eating dried meat in the day to avoid making fires. After his trapping days he acted as a guide for missionary and emigrant parties to Oregon, where he settled in 1844. Three years later he returned to Missouri and in 1849 died at Independence of the cholera. Contemporaries describe him as medium in height, with black hair, black whiskers and a very dark complexion, wiry and tough. The artist Jacob Miller spoke of his "face apparently composed of tan leather and whip cord, finished off with a peculiar blue-black tint, as if gunpowder had been burnt into his face."[40] Miller also remarks on Harris's talents as a campfire raconteur recounting his perilous experiences. Moses was often called "Black" or "Major" Harris. A fellow mountain man wrote his epitaph about him:

> Here lies the bones of old Black Harris
> who often traveled beyond the far west
> and for the freedom of Equal rights
> He crossed the snowy mountain heights
> Was free and easy kind of soul
> Especially with a Belly full[41]

The "Captain Stewart" mentioned in Ruxton's last paragraph may be Robert Stuart, born in Scotland in 1785, who migrated to Canada in 1807 and joined John Jacob Astor's Pacific Fur Company party, which founded Astoria in 1811. He led treks eastward across South Pass to St. Louis and eventually became a partner of Astor. He died in Detroit in 1834. His journal, published as *The Discovery of the Oregon Trail: Robert Stuart's Journal and Travelling Memoranda,* edited by Philip Ashton Rollins (1935), is judged an important western narrative second only to the journals of Lewis and Clark.[42]

In spite of the documentation for Harris and possibly Stewart, Ruxton's tale-setting seems more imaginary than factual. Harris's conversation with the lady in the St. Louis tavern is placed within a storytelling scene of mountain trappers on the trail preparing their supper of buffalo ribs, so that we have a tale-within-a-tale-within-a-novel, as George Ruxton's *Life in the Far West* has been labeled. The young English soldier-adventurer, who died at twenty-eight, cast his realistic adventures and intimate knowledge of the mountain men in semi-fictional form. So Harris's recital of the petrified forest yarn could have been heard by Ruxton and inserted into a hypothetical scene. Another western writer, Peter H. Burnett, the first governor of California, who listened to the "extraordinary stories" of the Rocky Mountain trappers and marveled at the "inventive talent" which produced the most "extravagant fiction," seems to support Ruxton's attribution of the petrified forest yarn to Harris:

> I knew in Missouri the celebrated Black Harris, as he was familiarly called, and was frequently in his company. He perhaps, invented the most extraordinary story of them all, and thenceforward he had no rival. He said that on one occasion he was hunting in the Rocky Mountains alone, and came in sight of what he supposed to be a beautiful grove of green timber; but, when he approached, he found it to be a petrified forest; and *so sudden* had been the process of petrifaction that the green leaves were all petrified, and the very birds that were then singing in the grove were also petrified in the act of singing, because their mouths were still open in their petrified state.[43]

But in the next sentence Burnett gives away the game, for he confesses: "This story I did not myself hear from Harris, but I learned it from good authority." A modern historian states that Harris almost certainly was not in St. Louis in 1823 but on the Yellowstone.[44]

So why did three western observers—James Clyman the mountain man, Frederick Ruxton the English soldier, and Peter Burnett the California governor—all credit Harris with delivering the fantasy of the petrified forest? So good a story, arising from Yellowstone's natural wonders, needed a proper peg, and Moses Harris, as a prototypical mountain man with the gift of trapper oratory, provided the peg. But in time an even more colorful and celebrated mountaineer, Jim Bridger, eclipsed Black Harris, as a greater hero absorbs a lesser, and the stream of Yellowstone yarns flowed toward Jim. So widespread was the legend of the petrified forest that Edgar Allan Poe alluded to it in "The Thousand-and-second Tale of Scheherazade," which concludes: "This account at first discredited, has been since corroborated by the discovery of a completely petrified forest near the Head waters of the Cheyenne, or Chienne River, which has its source in the Black Hills of the Rocky chain."[45]

The Glass Mountain

The shift from a petrified forest in Black Harris's telling to a petrified mountain in Bridger's rendition may have arisen from convergence with another favorite wonder in Jim's repertoire. He based this yarn on the Obsidian Cliff in Yellowstone Park, a spectacular mass of black volcanic glass that quickly became a tourist attraction. Chittenden relates how the scout literally bumped into the cliff on a hunting trip:

> Coming one day in sight of a magnificent elk, he took careful aim at the unsuspecting animal and fired. To his great amazement, the elk not only was not wounded, but seemed not even to have heard the report of the rifle. Bridger drew considerably nearer and gave the elk the benefit of his most deliberate aim; but with the same result as before. A third and a fourth effort met with a similar fate. Utterly exasperated, he seized his rifle by the barrel, resolved to use it as a club since it had failed as a firearm. He rushed madly toward the elk, but suddenly crashed into an immovable vertical wall which proved to be a mountain of perfectly transparent glass, on the farther side of which, still in peaceful security, the elk was quietly grazing. Stranger still, the mountain was not only of pure glass, but was a perfect telescopic lens, and, whereas, the elk seemed but a few hundred yards off, it was in reality twenty-five miles away![46]

Adapted from third person to first person and set in the convention of a dialogue between Munchausen and a credulous traveler, the tale takes on zest and immediacy:

> "Is there anything remarkable to be seen about here?" an inquisitive pilgrim asked him one day.
>
> "W-a-l-l," he replied, in a peculiar drawling tone, which he generally assumed in telling stories, in order to gain time to give his imagination fuller play, "there's a cur'ous mountain a few miles off'n the road, to the north of here, but the doggon'd trouble is you can't see the blamed thing."
>
> "A mountain and can't see it—that's curious," interrupted the pilgrim. "How large is it?"
>
> "Wall, I should say it's nigh onto three miles in circumference at the base, but its height is unknown," continued Bridger with imperturbable gravity.
>
> "Is it so high you can't see the top of it?" inquired the puzzled traveler.
>
> "That's what I say, stranger; you can't see the base of it either. Didn't you ever hear of the Crystal Mountain?"
>
> "I never did."
>
> "Wall, I'll tell you what it is. It's a mountain of crystal rock, an' so clear that the most powerful field glasses can't see it, much less the naked eye. You'll wonder, p'r'eps, how a thing that can't be seen no how was ever discovered. It came about in this way. You see, a lot of bones and the carcasses of animals an' birds was found scat-

tered all around the base. You see they ran or flew against this
invisible rock and jest killed themselves dead. You kin feel the rock
an' that's all. You can't see it. It's a good many miles high, for
everlastin' quantities of birds' bones are piled up all around the
base of it."[47]

The properties of Obsidian Cliff were remarkable enough without
Jim's adornments. To build a road along the cliff's base, Philetus W.
Norris heated the glassy stuff with fires and then poured cold water
on the fires to crack the cliff into fragments which could be cleared
away.[48]

Echo Mountain

Another natural wonder that Bridger converted to practical use
involved a distant mountain:

> Opposite a certain camping ground where he frequently stopped
> there arose the bald, flat face of a mountain, but so distant that the
> echo from any sound which originated in camp did not return for
> the space of about six hours. Bridger converted this circumstance
> into an ideal alarm clock. Upon retiring for the night he would call
> out hastily, "Time to get up!" and, true to his calculation, the alarm
> would roll back at the precise hour next morning when it was
> necessary for the camp to bestir itself.[49]

Some American tall tales revolved around echoes in natural settings. A dialect story enjoins that if a visitor goes to Echo Bay at the
head of Lake Superior and calls out "Hullo Yohnson," an echo will
come back fifteen minutes later, "Vich Yohnson?"[50]

Alum Creek

Not only mountains but streams and pools in Yellowstone inspired
natural wonder tales from the guide, as in his straightfaced report
on Alum Creek, here told in the third person:

> The origin of the name Alum Creek, a tributary of the Yellow-
> stone, was due to an accidental discovery by Bridger. One day he
> forded the creek and rode out several miles and back. He noticed
> that the return journey was only a small fraction of the distance
> going, and that his horse's feet had shrunk to mere points which

sank into the solid ground, so that the animal could scarcely hobble along. Seeking the cause he found it to be the astringent quality of the water, which was saturated with alum to such an extent that it had power to pucker distance itself.[51]

In a note to this wonder, the editors of a reprint edition of Chittenden's *Yellowstone National Park* cite two further references to the potent waters of Alum Creek. A traveler commented in his 1877 journal that "the headwaters of this stream are so strong with alum that one swallow is sufficient to draw one's face into such shape that it is almost impossible to get it straightened out again for one hour or so." This presumably true tall tale paved the way for exaggerative tall tales such as the following, credited to the publication *Truthful Lies,* and adopting the convention of the question-and-response conversation:

> "Driver, is it true that this water shrinks up things that get in it?" asks a credulous guidebook tourist as the coach was crossing Alum Creek.
> "True? Well, I guess yes! It used to be over seven miles from here to the Canyon hotel, but since they began sprinkling the road with water from this creek the distance has shortened up to three miles, as you will see if you watch the mile-posts."[52]

Hot Springs as Fireless Cookers

Another Yellowstone wonder that provided Bridger with eye-opening recitals lay on the west shore of Yellowstone Lake. Again Chittenden relates this "true" tale as an anecdote about Bridger:

> Somewhere along the shore an immense boiling spring discharges its overflow directly into the lake. The specific gravity of the water is less than that of the lake, owing probably to the expansive action of heat, and it floats in a stratum three or four feet thick upon the cold water underneath. When Bridger was in need of fish it was to this place that he went. Through the hot upper stratum he let fall his bait to the subjacent habitable zone, and having hooked his victim, cooked him *on the way out!*[53]

The hot springs of Arkansas have given rise to comparable yarns of farmers chasing hogs through the springs to scald them before butchering.[54]

The Great Salt Lake

Not only Yellowstone evoked Jim Bridger's truthful lies. The Great Salt Lake also inspired the guide, who used it for another natural way of preparing his meals. Colonel Henry Inman reports his marvel as he heard it directly from Jim:

> He told me and also many others, at various times, that in the winter of 1830 it began to snow in the valley of the Great Salt Lake, and continued for seventy days without cessation. The whole country was covered to a depth of seventy feet, and all the vast herds of buffalo were caught in the storm and died, but their carcasses were perfectly preserved.
> "When spring came, all I had to do," he declared, "was to tumble 'em into Salt Lake, an' I had pickled buffalo enough for myself and the whole nation for years!"
> He said that on account of that terrible storm, which annihilated them, there have been no buffalo in that region since.[55]

Again a foundation lay behind the seeming cock-and-bull story. An early explorer of the Great Salt Lake made the experiment of immersing a large piece of fresh beef in the lake for twelve hours and found it to be well corned. Thereafter he preserved all his beef by packing it into barrels without salt and filling them with lake water.[56]

In his *Type and Motif-Index of the Folktales of England and North America,* Ernest W. Baughman assigns a motif to "Remarkable salt content of water" (X1541*) and cites a Nevada example of a leaky pipe spraying water into a high wind and leaving only a shower of salt, so saline was the water.[57] The great snow of 1830 suggests the pivotal reference in Paul Bunyan tales to the Winter of the Blue Snow.

Pursued by Indians

A favorite yarn in Bridger's repertoire dealt not with natural wonders but with Indian fighting. It has come down to us in the storytelling frame, with Jim regaling his inquisitors who prod him for his adventures:

> "You must have had some curious adventures with, and hair-breadth escapes from the Indians, during your long life among

them," observed one of a party of a dozen or more, who had been relentlessly plying him with questions.

"Yes, I've had a few," he responded reflectively, "and I never to my dyin' day shall forget one in perticlar."

The crowd manifested an eager desire to hear the story. I will not undertake to give his words, but no story was ever more graphically told, and no throng of listeners ever followed a story's detail with more intense interest. He was on horseback and alone. He had been suddenly surprised by a party of six Indians, and putting spurs to his horse sought to escape. The Indians, mounted on fleet ponies, quickly followed in pursuit. His only weapon was a six-shooter. The moment the leading Indian came within shooting distance, he turned in his saddle and gave him a shot. His shot always meant a dead Indian. In this way he picked off five of the Indians, but the last one kept up the pursuit relentlessly and refused to be shaken off.

"We wus nearin' the edge of a deep and wide gorge," said Bridger. "No horse could leap over that awful chasm an' a fall to the bottom meant sartin death. I turned my horse suddint an' the Injun was upon me. We both fired to once, an' both horses wus killed. He now engaged in a han'-to-han' conflict with butcher knives. He was a powerful Injun—tallest I ever see. It was a long and fierce struggle. One moment I had the best of it, an' the next the odds wus agin me. Finally—"

Here Bridger paused as if to get breath.

"How did it end?" at length asked one of his breathless listeners, anxiously.

"The Injun killed me," he replied with slow deliberation.[58]

Here the scout has attached to himself a so-called catch tale popular with American raconteurs, in which the storyteller is killed in his own story—by wild animals (who in some versions bring a beaver to cut down a tree in which the man has taken refuge), by drowning, in a storm, or, as in Bridger's version, by Indians. Herbert Halpert collected a text of "The Indian Killed Me" (set in the Black Hills in Custer's time) in the New Jersey Pines in 1946, and he cites four other examples from printed and archival sources, in addition to Jim's recital. A constant feature of this catch tale is the storyteller's pause as he comes to the harrowing climax of his experience, with his escape dubious indeed; a listener, unable to contain himself, asks what happened next and is caught with the impossible terminus. In a version published in 1927, the cowboy artist Charles M. Russell has one storyteller attributing the yarn to another, Old Man Babcock, who concludes, "They killed me, b' God!"[59]

In the end Jim Bridger emerges as the mountain man Munchausen without peer. He absorbed lesser fabulists, like Black Harris, into his own legend, and came to represent in his person the whole breed of hardy trappers, scouts, and guides in the vast western wilderness. Fearless Indian fighter and expert trail-blazer, with a mountain pass named for him, Jim exemplified the virtues of the intrepid frontiersman from Boone to Carson. But he also possessed the comic lineaments of the Crockett tradition and gulled the tenderfoot with tales of Yellowstone's wonders, while providing subject matter for anecdotes others told of his discomfiture in the big city and antic behavior on his mountain turf. Writers like Ned Buntline and Emerson Hough enlarged Jim's fame. In American folklore he stands as the supreme Munchausen, enshrined in the epitaph: "Here lies Jim Bridger."

T W O

Oregon Smith

(1796–1893)

THE American Munchausen for whom we possess the fullest biography, collection, and analysis spent twenty-one years of his long life in Bloomington, Indiana, the oldest center for folklore studies in the United States. Half a century after his death, a folklorist at Indiana University found and followed his trail.

Abraham Smith was born in Tennessee, May 17, 1796. He homesteaded in Chrisman, Illinois, in 1832, emigrated to Oregon in 1852, returned east to Bloomington in 1859, and farmed there until he returned to Chrisman in 1881 to live with his daughter until his death in 1893. In both Bloomington and Chrisman he acquired a considerable reputation as a character and teller of large stories. Where as in southern Indiana he was familiarly known as Oregon Smith (because of the wondrous yarns he brought back about that state), residents of eastern Illinois seem not to have employed that cognomen but rather referred to him as Lying Abe, Uncle Abe, or Old Abe Smith. Both Hoosiers and Suckers did know him as Sassafras Smith and the Sassafras Doctor as a consequence of his medical prescriptions and testimonials to the powers of sassafras oil and ointment.

In his lifetime Lying Abe's celebrity did reach print. A piece about him in *The History of Edgar County, Illinois* in 1879 included two of his tales.[60] A novelist, C. Lauron Hooper, based the character Oregon

103

Abraham "Oregon" Smith

Roseberry, a legendary tale teller in a college town, upon Oregon
Smith in *A Cloverdale Skeleton,* published in New York in 1889.
Scholarly notice of Smith was first taken in 1942 by the folklorist
Herbert Halpert, then teaching at Indiana University, who learned
of the Oregon Smith tales from students collecting folklore in a class
assignment and published five of them in the *Southern Folklore
Quarterly.*[61] Two of the five narratives concerned Oregon and the
milk (from buffalo cows) which came out resembling butter. A third,
Smith's most celebrated story, told how he informed members of his
church he had shed barrels of tears over his weakness for stretching
the truth. Also in 1942 the first popularization of Oregon Smith
appeared, in a children's book of pseduo-folklore by Carl Carmer,

America Sings, which paraphrased the buffalo-milk yarn.[62] In the *Hoosier Folklore Bulletin* (1944) a fellow-folklorist of Halpert's at Indiana University, William Hugh Jansen, presented "More on Oregon Smith"[63] and followed this up in 1948 with an article in *Hoosier Folklore* on "Lying Abe: A Teller and His Reputation."[64] This piece was abstracted from Jansen's doctoral dissertation, accepted the following year in the English department at Indiana University under the direction of Stith Thompson, just before Thompson inaugurated a doctoral program in folklore. Jansen's dissertation, "Abraham 'Oregon' Smith, Pioneer, Folk Hero and Tale-Teller," a manuscript of 354 pages, embodied a corpus of 82 tales (ten not linked to Smith) plus variants, along with six chapters of biography eked out in tedious detail from slender records, and two on oral folk-memory of Smith and his narrative art. The dissertation was reproduced in book form, unamended save for a new preface from Jansen, by Arno Press in 1977. In the course of his researches Jansen interviewed thirty-nine informants, chiefly in Bloomington and Chrisman, and obtained other information by correspondence and from court records and private papers.

Life and Legend

One county history credits Abraham Smith's lineage to John Smith.[65] Little is known of Abraham's first twenty-five years in Tennessee, save that he came of Quaker stock. In 1821 he moved briefly to Hendricks County, Indiana, and associating with Indians there, gleaned much about roots and herbs which he would later incorporate into his medical preparations. Moving back and forth between Indiana and Illinois, he homesteaded three times. One surviving document from 1850 in which Smith, self-styled the "Orator," files for divorce against Eunice Poland, his wife whom he had discovered to be already married, gives some flavor of Abraham's temperament and rhetoric. The suit states that he wed Eunice in Covington, Indiana, in 1849 and passed two pleasant months with her, during which she cared for his children by his first, deceased wife.

> But lo: to the great misfortune and misery of your Orator the scene changed. The hitherto placid and obliging Eunice became the vexation and torment of his life. . . . Her tongue became as

if envenomed with the poison of the *copperhead*. She drove
all peace and concord from his house. . . . She would leave your
Orator's bed and lay in some other part of the house and then
scold all night like a Fury permitting no one to rest about the
house. . . . At last she had the unblushing affrontery [*sic*] to swer
[*sic*] that she had another husband living.[66]

Although the disposition of the case if not recorded, Jansen con-
jectures that the Court declared the marriage invalid.

For the Oregon years little record exists, although the Paris, Illinois *Prairie-Beacon,* the only newspaper in Edgar County while
Smith was living there from 1848–1852, regularly printed glowing
accounts of the Oregon country. Presumably in Oregon he farmed,
practiced medicine, and on a side trip prospected in California. On
his return to Bloomington in 1859 he enlarged his repertoire with
Oregon wonders.

In Bloomington, Smith acquired land and some means. Folk memory recalls his involvement with the Christian Church, from which
he withdrew when one faction wished to introduce an organ, which
other members, including Smith, considered an instrument of the
devil. He donated a lot for the new First Church of Christ to be built
on, around 1880, and it was derisively called the Sassafras Church
by the opposition, to link it with Smith's eccentricity. Also at this
time he was hauled into court on the charge of "laying rude and
angry hands" upon a pregnant woman and attempting to strike her
with a hatchet. Apparently Abraham, who was then eighty-five, was
trying to repossess goods from an unwilling tenant. The case seems
to have been settled out of court. A year later, after his second wife's
death, he removed to Illinois to live with various relatives for his
last twelve years.

From this last period there survives a handbill distributed by
Smith at the age of ninety, revealing to the world his secret recipe
for sassafras oil, with an extensive list of the illnesses it could cure,
including catarrh, pneumonia, heart disease, scarlet fever, and can-
cer. He claimed to have made and used it himself for seventy years
and to have cured fifteen hundred people, some of whose names he
appended, with the oil. Even at his advanced age, his zeal for doctoring is seen in his storming out of his daughter's house, when she
refused to give him money to go to Chicago to practice medicine as
he was nearing eighty-nine, and doing the same at the Jarvis home

because they would not let him treat their sick baby with sassafras oil. In addition he wished to pick up the child by the heels and shake it to unchoke it from the croup. In those last years he boarded around and at age ninety ran off in his carriage with the grass widow, who fifty years his junior, worked for one of his grand-nephews. His grandsons hastened after him and fetched him home. In 1888 he entered into the last of his many lawsuits, this one lasting three and a half years and being directed against his daughter Deborah Littlefield for breach of contract in failing to support him as agreed to. In response she countered that he "was subject to violent fits of passion and rage," used abusive language, and accused her of trying to poison him with "Rough on Rats." Ultimately the case was dismissed, the year before his death. To the end he was remembered as a talker. One of his landlords complained, "You couldn't have strangers come in because he would consume all the time." The daughter of the landlady remembered, "Just as long as anybody'd set up and talk, he'd talk too." He did not live to the century mark, dying of Bright's disease at ninety-seven. An obituary called him "the most remarkable personage that ever lived in Edgar County."[67] The terms most frequently applied to him by his biographer Jansen, in the light of his constant litigation, are "irascible" and "contentious."

The Repertoire

The 72 narratives and their variants connected with Abe Smith may be categorized in several ways: by printed and oral sources, by Indiana and Illinois informants, by genres of tall tales and anecdotal legends, and by such themes as the strong man, the sassafras doctor, the Oregonian, and the general exaggerator.

Printed and Oral Sources

Fourteen tales in the recovered corpus appear in the 1879 Illinois local history, H. W. Beckwith's *History of Vermilion County,* and the 1889 novel, C. Lauron Hooper's *A Cloverdale Skeleton.* All but three of this group, published during Abe's lifetime, were recovered in mid-twentieth century oral tradition and so document the tenacity of the cycle on the lips of Abe and his successor storytellers who preserved his tales. Both the history and the novel include variants

of the most popular tale in the canon, "Carrying the Heavy Burden,"
found in twenty versions, five more than are recorded for the next
most popular tale. The county history source must date from before
1851 (when Smith departed Illinois for Oregon), since he then returned to Indiana and did not come back to Illinois until 1881, two
years after the history's publication. This printed narrative then
gains our interest from its age, originating in the 1840s, from its
popularity, from the evidence in the preamble of Smith's yarnspinning reputation, and for the opportunity to contrast printed and oral
styles of folktale rendition.

CARRYING THE HEAVY BURDEN

It is said that Smith was a little peculiar in some respects, one
of his peculiarities being in the marvelous yarns which he told
in regard to himself. Among numerous other stories the following is a fair sample from his prolific brain:

"Some years before moving to these parts," he relates, "I was
living in a small town in Tennessee. One night, just about the
time I was thinking of retiring, suddenly the cry of fire re-
sounded through the streets, and all outside was commotion and
alarm. Quicker than it takes to tell it, I had jerked on my boots
and, without hat or coat, was at the scene of destruction. I never
knew, before that night, how strong I was. Excitement sometimes paralyzes a man; but, in my case, it seems rather to add
strength, or at least to bring out whatever I possess. I saw at
once that it was my friend's hardware store, and my friendship
to him seemed rather to add to the excitement. Without stopping
a moment to think, I ran into the burning building and seized
upon the first object that met my sight. I seized and carried it
out and across the street; and then I realized what I had done.
The burden which I had carried was a bag of shot, and by actual
measurements there were in the bag four bushels of shot. After-
ward it was discovered that where I had trod on the brick pave-
ment the bricks were considerably sunken in the ground, from
the great weight that lay on my shoulders. I could scarcely believe it myself, but, as several persons had seen the feat performed, there could be no doubt."[68]

The reproduction of Smith's words in this personal narrative of a
herculean feat gives an impression of verisimilitude, but the language is literary and lacks idiomatic flavor. Yet the image of the
storyteller as strong hero in his own tale certainly conforms to the

oral legend. In the novel Hooper singles out the key motif for a brief reference that does also include Smith's words, ironically spoken:

> Once he had carried on his shoulder a beam of wood one foot wide, one foot thick and fifty feet long, the weight being so great as to sink him into the earth to his knees at every step. "Ain't nigh as strong now as I used to was," said he.[69]

One of the leading storytellers in Chrisman to inherit Lying Abe's mantle, Guy Scott, similarly repeats some of Smith's words in his version, but with a comic twist:

> There's lots of stories about his strength. Some of them he told himself. Others people made up about him. He was awful stout, now. So there was reason for the stories. This one I know he told himself, I heard him.
>
> Up there at Danville there was a store where you bought shot, powder, caps, and all such stuff. It was all muzzle-loaders in his day, of course. One night there was a fire in this hardware store and Abe was in town. He claimed he knew there was a great deal of ammunition in the hardware store. So he wanted to carry it out and get it away from the fire. It was burning fast. So he filled a bed sack with shot. Here he came out of the fire with a bed sack over his shoulder with eight bushels of shot in it. It was so heavy he sank into the stone pavement at every step.
>
> He said, "They told a lie on me about that fire. They said I sank in the pavement up to my knees. That wasn't true. It was only up to my ankles. The tracks is there yet." he'd say. "The tracks is there yet."[70]

This oral text delivered in 1947 follows closely the plot line of the 1879 county history version, save that the fire in the earlier account is in Tennessee and in the later in Danville, Illinois, but the phrasing of Guy Scott is far more direct and natural, as befits an oral telling. Smith's turning the charge of lying against his detractors by reducing the exaggeration sets this variant apart from straightforward solemn asseverations. What is factual in the narrative is the prefatory statement about Abe Smith's strength and the stories, his own and others, to which it gave rise. The motif of "Sinking in a hard surface"[71] is widely reported in American folklore and gets attached to Jones Tracy, on Mount Desert Island, Maine, who also carried a load of shot from an ammunition store that caused him to sink into a cement sidewalk. As with Abe Smith, Tracy's tracks are

said to be still visible.[72] A complementary motif, "Strong man carries
a giant load,"[73] characterizes serious annals of the strong hero, and
this element of possible veracity adds piquancy to the Abe Smith
legend.

Indiana and Illinois Traditions

Abe Smith created legendary traditions in both Monroe County,
Indiana, and Edgar County, Illinois; however, the two traditions
followed entirely independent courses. Jansen found the Illinois tradition considerably stronger, as a result of its later chronological
period and the fact that expert raconteurs emerged in Chrisman to
carry on Abe's stories. Also after his retirement to Illinois, Abe had
more time to spend loafing in downtown gathering places. Only a
half dozen tales, less than ten percent of the full stock of Abe's
known hoard, were collected in both states, with over twice as many
separate tales, 55 to 21, reported from Illinois as from Indiana. The
great point of difference between the two veins of storytelling is the
emphasis on Oregon marvels in southern Indiana folk memory, leading to the appellation "Oregon" Smith, and the low incidence of this
aspect in eastern Illinois. Perhaps by the time Smith moved from
Indiana to Illinois after his Oregon sojourn the allure of that far
western paradise had faded. But in Bloomington in the 1940s people
still remembered Abe Smith's tales from the 1860s and 70s about
Oregon where oranges grew as large as watermelons, berries as
large as apples, and turnips as large as pumpkins, and where the
rain did not wet the people it fell on; hence the expression among
Hoosiers in southern Indiana, "You lie like Oregon Smith."

The most original of the Oregon tall tales, without known parallels, but recorded in the 1889 novel and in two oral variants, deals
with "buffalo milk butter."

Buffalo Milk Butter

One time when I was out in Oregon walkin along the foot of a
hill, I came to a little cold stream. About half way across I started
noticing little bits of yaller stuff floating on the top of the water,
and a bit further on down I saw a small pool of pale yaller churn-
ing around slowly. Well now, that interested me considerable.

I looked at it and then, thinks I, it won't hurt none to taste the stuff. Well, I did and, do you know, it tasted just like butter— unsalted butter.

Such a curious thing kinda got my dander up, and I decided to investigate. I looked around and didn't see nothin', so I started to climb up the side of the hill that the stream was flowing down. I clumb and I clumb till finally I come up over a little rise, and there was a herd of buffalo cows a-standin' in a wide spot in the stream to keep cool.

They was packed close and was stamping right smart to keep the flies off. They was packed so clost together and a-stompin' so hard that the milk was squirtin' outa their bags and a-flowin' into the water. There was so much of it a-runnin' over the rocks that it churned itself on the way down, and the cold water made it gather at the bottom of the hill. Yes sir, there was a mighty practical way to get good clean butter going to waste right there in the wilds of Oregon.[74]

In a related whopper, a unique text without variants either in the Smith cycle or in general, Abe told a bunch of students about a bob-tailed cow he had owned in Oregon who gave milk that was near butter. When a student asked why the bobbed tail was significant, Abe had his answer: "Well, sir," he said, "that's it! The sun shined in so hot where her tail shoulda been that when the milk hit the pail it was all curdled and ready for churnin'."[75] These butter tales, special in Oregon Smith's repertoire, stand in contrast to stock lies he placed in Oregon, such as "Shingling on the Fog," "Lying Contest" ("The Big Kettle to Cook the Big Turnip"), and "False Mixed Weather" ("Flight from the Bear in Berry-Picking Time on the Frozen River") in which Smith is said to have run from a bear for three and a half months, eating berries, until winter came. Abe Smith's telling of Oregon tales eventually led to the best known of all tales about him in Bloomington, his censure by his church for this propensity to stretch the truth. Six variants are on record: one from Hooper's novel of 1889; one from the local newspaper, the *Bloomington World Telephone* for November 23, 1944, in an article by B. W. Bradfute recalling "Old Bloomington;" one collected by Emma Lou Robinson while a student at Indiana University in 1940; and three collected by Jansen in Bloomington in 1944. The following version, from an informant of Jansen, is unique in including examples of the stories for which he was chastised. Ironically Smith was one of the founders of the First Church of Christ in Bloomington which now interrogated him.

Oregon Smith Is Churched

Anyway, Hughes, Bray and some others in the church felt they had to do something to make the church better and brighter, and so they decided to weed the tares from the wheat. And Oregon was one who was supposed to be a teller of tales; so they churched him. You know that churching was? They'd call a sinner before the officials of the church and charge him and make him admit his faults.

They charged that he had told that the ground in Oregon was so rich that when they planted pumpkins, the vines would be so rank they'd haul the pumpkins along over the ground and bruise them all up.

The other story they churched him for was about the fog in Oregon and know thick it was. And it is thick, I've seen it, just rolls in, thick as it could be. Well, it rolled in so thick once that two men who were shingling a roof shingled right on over the edge of the house and went on putting a roof on the fog.

Then he also said that he found a hot water spring—that's what we'd call a geyser—that you could boil eggs in, it was so hot. Now, we know that's true, but the community there was ignorant.

There might have been more stories that they cited; but he agreed he may have been wrong, and he said he had just shed barrels and barrels of tears over it—barrels and barrels.[76]

Three very popular American tall tales are incorporated here. All over the United States fast growing vines—pumpkin, melon, squash—drag fruit along the ground and wear them out before they ripen.[77] And all over the United States men shingle beyond the roof in a thick fog.[78] Tall-tale heroes who annex this exploit include John Darling, Gib Morgan, and Jones Tracy. The geyser that cooks eggs was one of Jim Bridger's true tales that he joined to inflated tales when people would not believe him. But in the "Barrels of Tears" anecdote, the point is not the previous tall tales that Oregon Smith committed but his telling another exaggeration in the act of repentance, and the other variants play with this conceit. One text gives this comment by a deacon present: "Even one barrel of tears is too many tears for the record." Another, that of the novel *The Cloverdale Skeleton*, has an elder remonstrating, and Smith lowering his barrels to buckets and finally conceding, "Well, brethren, mebbe I never shed no tears about it, but I've thought a heap over it and it's made me *feel* powerful bad."[79]

This story is not in itself a tall tale but an amusing anecdote about Abe Smith's trait of releasing tall tales, and since folk memory in Bloomington revealed distrust of the exaggerator, or liar, and suspicion of Abe's character, the anecdote could be true. The church could well take the liar to task. But barrels and barrels of tears were also shed by repenting liars (so they informed church boards) in Massachusetts in 1902 and Vermont in 1934, and the Vermont poet Walter Hard captures another sinner who sold cattle on the Sabbath and thus expressed his remorse in church: "Wal, I will say I'm sorry it was Sunday when I sold them cattle."[80] So what we have in this circumstantial narrative about Smith's being "churched"—a folk ritual in itself—is a floating legend that has hooked on to an appropriate personality. This legend never surfaced in Illinois, in spite of the more vigorous recollection of Lying Abe there, perhaps because Edgar County felt no disapproval as did Monroe County of drawing the long bow.

As "Barrels of Tears" is the most popular Abe Smith tale in southern Indiana, so is "Carrying the Heavy Burden" (already given) the most popular in eastern Illinois, and as the Oregon tales endure in Bloomington, so do the doctor tales thrive in Chrisman. "Barrels of Tears" is directly related to the Oregon experience, but "Carrying the Heavy Burden," emphasizing Smith's strength as well as his mendacity, does not link with the narratives about Smith's quackery. Doctoring became Abe's main activity in his retirement years in Illinois, when he had given up homesteading, and would naturally lend itself to legend formation. But Indiana too recalls the Sassafras Doctor, and a trickle of the Oregon experiences survives in Illinois, so the two traditions do overlap.

Tall Tales and Anecdotal Legends

Abe Smith stories fall into two main genres: the exaggerative tales he told (many about himself) and the comic anecdotes others told about him. These categories slide into each other at points, for Abe did possess superior strength that lent some credence to his boasts and gave rise to legends of his feats, and the same narrative could be in one instance Abe's tall tale and in another a hero-worshiper's legendary report. An example can be seen in the story of "Beating the Bully," recorded in five variants as a true event told about Abe Smith. But one teller, a grandson of Abe's, states: "I asked Grandfather about it and he told me it was true. I heard him tell it many times." Is this another of Abe's lies or a veracious, if remarkable, statement?

BEATING THE BULLY

Well, that cross road just south of town where the gas stations are was a place they used to race horses and hold muster. You know Grandfather raised horses. Well, Grandfather had the name of being a purty good man, and there was a bully come over from Indiany to whip him. This bully asked for Abe Smith.
Grandfather said, "I'm Abe Smith."
The bully said, "I've come to whip you."
"Oh," he says "I'm too good-natured to fight." He talked him out of it, you see.
After a while the bully came up a second time and said, "If you're Abe Smith, I'm going to fight you."
Grandfather said, "No, I don't enjoy fighting," and he talked him out of it again.
Then the bully came after him a third time. Grandfather said, "No. A man'd have to spit right in my face I reckon before I'd fight with him."
Before he'd finished the bully spit right in his face, and Grandfather went after him and nearly killed him. Grandfather about kicked his head off.[81]

At the time that he collected this yarn, Jansen could not know of counterpart legends which have since come to light. On the Maine coast in 1956, I recorded "How Barney Beal Awed the Bully of Peak's Island." In this case the bully who had come to challenge strong man Barney Beal of Beal's Island departed abruptly without fighting when he saw Barney pick up a five hundred pound water barrel and drink out of the bunghole.[82] In the Upper Peninsula of Michigan in 1946, I heard accounts of tough woodsmen who walked long distances to fight braggarts and bullies.[83] In Afro-American folk legendary a spectacular fight between the strongest slaves of rival plantations is arranged by their masters, and one frightens the other into withdrawing by a real or mock display of awesomeness.[84] In Japan one mighty wrestler travels a long distance to challenge the great champion and is discomfited at seeing the champion point to his home with a plow or the champion's mother lift a big brazier with one hand which the challenger cannot budge.[85]

This legend-complex takes two main forms: the strong hero besting the challenger (although with the northern woodsmen the challenger is the hero), or the hero frightening the challenger away (and sometimes as with the Afro-American subform becoming a trickster-hero). In another tale which Jansen fails to relate to "Beating the Bully," Abe Smith did intimidate a challenger who came looking for him, by pretending to be his own brother and picking up a plow to point to Abe in the distance—an exploit also credited to Jones Tracy. Abe also lifted a full whiskey barrel and drank out of the bung, although in that telling, the deed came after he had knocked out two fellows in a brawl. Again in a separate narrative Abe knocks down bullies at a revival meeting, usually by kicking. References to his kicking abilities occur in "Beating the Bully," as in this variant: "Abe jumped up in the air and, with his two feet at once, kicked him [a contentious horseman] so hard that he knocked him straight out in the street. And Abe, he landed back on his feet again."[86] Other anecdotal memories recall his kicking ability, even as he neared ninety: kicking a hat out of man's hand extended over his head or jumping into the air and cracking his heels twice before landing. Some of these feats are connected with a French-Canadian strong hero, Joe Mouffron, who pointed with a plow and could kick up to the ceiling.

The interlacing of fact and fancy, exaggerative tale and migratory legend is well exemplified in the family of tales revolving around the bully's challenge. Lifting, kicking, fighting, bragging all characterize the Munchausen strong hero.

Liar, Strong Hero, Doctor

The themes of Abe Smith stories celebrate his talents in three directions: as drawer of long bows, as a modern Heracles, and as an herb doctor. Combining the roles of Munchausen and strong hero is not uncommon among American storytellers, who often direct their exaggerations to their physical might, and we have seen examples of Abe's stories in both these veins, as a spinner of windies about giant fruits and vegetables and as a celebrant of his powers of lifting and fighting. The strong hero could and did exist in folk legend quite apart from the Munchausen hero, and the latter might yarn about the former. As one of Jansen's informants put it: "In those days men took a lot of pride in their strength. Different fellows would compete among themselves and with any strangers in town. Every community had a strong man and a fighter.[87] According to folk testimony Abe did indeed possess an uncommon physique and local renown for lifting heavy burdens, as well as for being a great talker.

But Abe departs from his fellow-Munchausens and strong men in his doctoring role, which he took with utmost seriousness, although his fellow-townsmen generally regarded him as a quack and referred to him as a "sassafras-oil doctor." Tales of Dr. A. Smith," as he styled himself on his handbills, again cross the genres, for he told lies about his medical cures, while many informants relished giving anecdotal descriptions of how Abe made his sassafras oil. A favorite fiction Lying Abe related of his doctoring finds him operating on his wife.

REPLACING HIS WIFE'S LIVER

He claimed he performed the first surgery done in these parts. His patient was his wife: she had something wrong with her insides. This was in the summer. Of course he didn't have many instruments, maybe not any. This was all before he started that sassafras oil stuff.

Anyhow he took his wife and laid her out on the grass. Then he took his knife out of his pocket, opened it, and wiped off the blade. Then he opened up his wife. He took her entrails out and spread them on the grass. He was looking them over to find out what the trouble was. He had forgot about an old sow that was wandering around the place. You know, pigs are crazy after blood. She came snorting up and grabbed a mouthful of guts. Before Abe could stop her she had tore them in two and run off.

He was desperate. He looked around quick and saw an old ewe standing across the fence. He ran over, picked her up in his two hands like that [arms extended stiff and fingers digging deep in the imaginary wool] and lifted her across the fence. He threw that ewe down besides his wife and opened it up. He yanked out the entrails of the ewe and put them in his wife. He knew there was nothing the matter with them, the ewe was healthy enough. Then he sewed up his wife and took her in and laid her on the bed.

He used to say she got along all right after the operation. Of course she passed sheep manure all that winter. And she had a

lamb the next spring. But she was really all right after that except
that she always had a hankering for grass.[88]

Eleven variants of this wonder are on record. In one Abe tells the
tale in front of his wife, who claims it never happened, whereupon
he remarked, "Mother, you were so sick, you just didn't know what
was going on." Actually Smith here has delivered a version of a
European folktale, one of the Grimms' Märchen, only once before
reported in the United States, which he has appropriated to
himself.[89]

In another fictional doctoring tale, Abe offered to cure a chap of a
running sore which had not healed. Abe tied him to the ground, set
a kettle full of lard over a roaring fire, and then poured dippers of
boiling lard on the fellow's sore, while the patient screamed to
heaven. "There," said Abe, "now he has a burn and I know how to
treat that. Yeah, I'm hell on burns."[90] A similar treatment is ascribed
to Johnny Appleseed.

When it came to claims for the curative properties of his sassafras
oil, however, the self-styled doctor turned dead serious. Ironically,
his audiences half-swallowed some of his lies and looked askance at
his assertion of the virtues in his oil. Fellow townsmen in Chrisman
described in close detail how Abe manufactured his remedy. The
equipment consisted of a big flat sandstone rock with a hole drilled
through it on one corner and a pipe running through the hole. Abe
cut dried sassafras rails (which his son-in-law brought in from his
farm) into small chunks and packed them into a big iron kettle so
tightly that he could turn the kettle over without spilling any. Then
he placed the kettle upside down on the rock over the hole and
cemented the edges down tight. Next he built a hot fire against the
kettle. After a while the sassafras began to distill and a trickle of
black oil issued from the hole. From that oil he made his medicine.
"Imagine getting any oil out of of that dried timber," marveled one
citizen of Chrisman, who did praise the oil for curing catarrh.[91]
Another recollects Abe attending an Old Settlers Reunion in a park
where he was introduced as the oldest man in eastern Illinois. He
promptly took the speaker's stand (elegant in his split-tail coat),
reached in his tail pocket and brought forth a bottle of his sassafras
oil. Then in a singsong voice he recited his spiel: "I got to manufacturing this here sassafras oil. I want to tell you it will cure the

gravel in your bladder. A few doses of this and it will run from you like mud." And he alluded to testimonials to support his statement.[92] Finally the bystanders persuaded him to relinquish the stand in favor of a singing group.

Thus the picture of Dr. A. Smith in his last years, a W. C. Fields figure touting his cure-all. The oral accounts of his sassafras still echo closely the details provided in Abe's handbill, which the speakers state they never saw. This handbill, printed in 1885 or 1886, must have functioned much as did a broadside ballad in relation to oral ballads, by stabilizing and reinforcing the tradition.

Style and Appearance

Contemporary observation and folk memory have left clear impressions of Abe Smith's narrative style and manner. Acquaintances describe him as tall, rawboned, broadshouldered, about one hundred and seventy pounds, smooth-shaven, rosy-cheeked, with a high-pitched, resonant voice. Before beginning a story he cleared his throat in a peculiar way. A photograph in old age shows a surprisingly handsome man with alert eyes, a fair amount of gray white hair, and a ruddy complexion, imposing and impressive in a three-piece suit, bow tie, white collar and his inevitable cane clutched in his left hand.

As a narrator, according to Jansen, he possessed a fairly fixed and restricted repertoire, devoid of smut, and demanded full attention from his circle, not deigning to engage in lying contests. He would sit on a barrel or an easy chair in one of the stores and entertain young and old with his stories. Loafing was a legitimate part of life in the horse and buggy days, and respectable citizens spent "loafing time" in the barber shop or grocery store as part of their daily routine; into this milieu Lying Abe regally fitted. Accounts tell of his holding forth on a street corner or coming across a field where the workers would stop him and request a yarn. He delivered the tallest whoppers with an air of deep conviction which led some listeners to believe that Abe had fallen prey to his own fantasies. If some youth smiled or giggled, Smith quelled him with "What's so funny about that, son?" His hands moved continually and his shrill old man's voice reverberated. One commentator contrasted Lying Abe with Honest Abe Lincoln, who told stories to illustrate a point, while

Smith always made himself the hero. Both were well known in eastern Illinois and must have met. Some in Abe Smith's circle remarked on his false teeth that clattered, but which did not inhibit his flow. In adapting folktales in general circulation to his own persona and convincing his listeners that these were his invented tales, the sassafrass doctor rendered, according to Jansen, a "creative narrative performance," the most memorable his region had ever beheld.[93]

THREE

John Darling

(1809–1903 [?])

ANOTHER tall-tale hero, long-lived like Abe Smith, cut and rafted timber in the Catskill Mountains in the southwestern bump of the state of New York. Now that the heyday of the lumber industry is over, this area has become known as the borscht circuit because of the popularity of Jewish resort hotels filled by vacationers from New York City. But old woodsmen and raftsmen living on the fringes of the resort towns in Sullivan and Delaware Counties remember with awe the tale-telling of one of their number, John Darling. "He was the damndest liar in seven states," said one. "He was one of the biggest damn liars ever walked," said another. "My grandfather'd say, 'You know that's a lie!' and John would say, 'No, it ain't! It's a fact.' "[94]

The publication of the Catskill Munchausen's tales commenced in the 1930s as folklorists and writers discovered and mined his vein. In 1935, Mildred Tyler, longtime resident of Sullivan County, placed an article entitled "John Darling, Teller of Tall Tales" in a regional magazine that was published briefly out of Troy, New York, *The Half Moon*. Carl Carmer, the professor-turned-author after his success with his book of local folkways, *Stars Fell on Alabama,* used four of these tales in 1937 in a volume of rewritten hero-legends for youngsters, *The Hurricane's Children,* in which he added a spurious concoction making Darling an Erie Canal boatman enamored of a

Johnny Darling swinging a 500-pound deer.

redheaded cook. This extraneous addition he omitted in re-using the tales in 1940 in *Listen for a Lonesome Drum,* his attempt to duplicate his Alabama coup for New York. Also in 1940 Harold W. Thompson printed seven John Darling lies, brought to him by Mildred Tyler, in his collection of New York State folklore, *Body, Boots and Britches.* In 1941 in a juvenile book of American fakelore heroes, *Yankee Doodle's Cousins* by Anne Malcolmson, John Darling led off the parade with the same stories given by Carmer, down to the Erie Canal redhead. Reasserting his claim, Carmer printed his tales in a third book in 1942, *America Sings,* apparently aimed at still younger readers, but this time eschewing the redhead.

The best and fullest sampling of the cycle, for the first time meeting professional standards of literal texts, named informants, contextual data, and comparative notes, appeared in 1944 in an article by Herbert Halpert, "John Darling, a New York Munchausen," presenting twenty-one texts. Of these, two had previously been attached to Darling by both Carmer and Thompson, and two others by Carmer alone.

A year later a New York City writer of juvenile folklore, Moritz

The Cherry-Tree Buck

Jagendorf, sketched the biography of "Catskill Darling: Facts about a Folk Hero," in the *New York Folklore Quarterly*. The nebulous figure took on flesh and personality. Darling's parents had originally emigrated from Scotland and settled in Sullivan County, New York, where John was born in 1809. Besides his work in the woods and rafting down the Delaware River, he tried his hand at farming and in 1869 purchased a farm on the banks of Sand Pond, now a popular summer resort. Neighbors referred to him as the Sage of Sand Pond. The mortgage was foreclosed in 1883, and the next year John was admitted to Middletown Homeopathic Hospital, and thence to the Sullivan County poorhouse, where he died in 1893 (some sources say 1903). A journalist, who as a boy remembered seeing him, commented that Darling "looked like a Rip Van Winkle as he sauntered from the woods. He was known as John Cicero Caesar Augustus Darling, as that was the name he applied to himself."[95] Another description pictures Darling as a thin little man with long whitish hair and squinty blue eyes who wore cowhide boots or walked barefoot and carried a black carved stick.[96] One Delaware County oldtimer referred to John as a great preacher who went from one schoolhouse to another preaching the gospel.[97]

No fresh field-collected tales were added to the John Darling cycle after Halpert's article, although in 1949 Jagendorf devoted a booklength juvenile to the Catskill hero.[98]

The known corpus of tales depicts Darling as a hunter, farmer, and woodsman. In eight of Halpert's texts—all short and anecdotal—John is out hunting, and tells such familiar feats as shooting a deer with cherry pits which grew the following year into little cherry trees (a Baron Münchhausen specialty); the lucky shot that nets a deer, a pickerel, and a honey tree; and the slow-burning powder in his gun which took the ball he fired a day to catch up with the deer. In four tales he is working on the farm: plowing, cradling oats, building a barn. John's most repeated wonder, reported in three variants by Halpert and included by both Carmer and Thompson, concerns a sow on his farm.

THE SOW AND THE CART

He said, "I had a nice sow pig. I thought the world of her. Wanted to keep her." Said, "One day she jumped over a fence and broke her back." So he says, "I thought first I'd knock her in the head." Then he says, "I thought I wouldn't kill her; I'd let her live as long as she could; I'd let her die herself." And he says, "I got a-thinkin' maybe I could fix something to put under her so she could get her hind parts along." So he says, "I went and built a cart—two-wheeled cart." Says, "I put that under her and strapped that cart fast so it would stay." And he said, "She was around there for quite a while, and I fed her." Said, "One day I got up and she was gone—away." Said, "I thought that old pig had went off somewheres and died." Said, "I got up one morning 'long in the fall; it was quite cold." Said, "I looked up on the hill, and I saw that old sow comin' down the hill." Said, "She's so fat she could hardly waller." And he said, "She had ten nice pigs," he said, "and, by God, each pig had a cart."[99]

In American tall-tale lore other creatures also transmit their acquired appendages to their offspring. Bear cubs are born with butter casks on their tails, fawns with red flannel ribbons on their horns, baby partridges with sweaters in place of feathers.[100] The following tale is another farming event with wide repercussions.

STOUT PANTS AND THE SPLIT STUMP

John Darling was out breakin' up some new ground, and he had seven yoke of oxen hooked to the plow. He said, "Them oxen got scared at somethin'!" And he said they made a beeline right down across that new ground there. He said he aimed that plow for a great big oak stump, he said, and it split that stump right in two, and jerked him and the plow right through. He said the stump closed up and ketched him right by the seat of the pants. He said he hung on them plow handles, and they broke the hull seven yokes and left him there. The only way he could get out was to climb out of his pants.[101]

Tracy Jones related a similar experience befalling him on Mount Desert Island; Paul Bunyan and Babe the Blue Ox pull up the stump.

As a lumberjack John Darling told of a big tree in the state of Washington which he tried to cut down, only to find four other fellows had been working two weeks on the other side, and of a gooseberry tree from which he picked thousands of gooseberries and cut a hundred cord of wood. One surprising adventure that befell him in the woods takes a different turn from these conventional lies about giant plants.

STRETCHING IN THE NIGHT

John Darling was quite a man. One time John says he was down in the woods and he got lost. And uh—it was dark, come dark on him, and all at oncet he fell off from a ledge o' rocks. And as he went through the air, he says, "I turned around fast enough so I ketched me toes at the edge o' the rock, and hung there till morning. The ledge was about fourteen feet high and in the morning my head was within about six inches of the ground." He'd stretched out during the night hanging there.[102]

Little information survives on the narrative technique of the Sage of Sand Pond, save that he loved to match stories with the boys in the barroom, or tell them to youngsters in the home, with a deadly earnest mien. "Somebody would set down and tell a story that *could* be true, and he'd set down and tell one on the same order—and ten times worse."[103] In his declining years in the poorhouse Darling was thought to be insane and a teller of crazy stories. His keepers would be surprised to learn that posterity thinks of him as a folk hero.

FOUR

Gib Morgan

(1842–1909)

$\mathcal{T}$HE biographer of Gilbert Morgan, Mody C. Boatright, called him "the most fertile creator of comic folktales known to America" and labeled him "the Munchausen of the Oil Fields."[104] We would certainly agree, for the great majority of the fifty-one tales placed on record by Mody Boatright are unique, in our present knowledge, and not to be found in the repertoires of other tall-tale heroes. They constitute elaborate adventures and inventions Gib Morgan told on himself as oil driller in several American states and in foreign lands. To Boatright, a folklorist at the University of Texas who served as chairman of their English department, goes the credit for collecting yarns attributed to Gib by oil field workers and publishing them, with a biographical account of Gib, in 1945.

A curious prehistory of the unveiling of the tall-tale hero dates from 1930, when Frank Shay published the first attempt at assembling an American folk pantheon in *Here's Audacity! American Legendary Heroes* and included "Kemp Morgan, the Texas Oil Driller." Shay's gallery actually presented mainly fake heroes in the mold of Paul Bunyan, conspicuously present of course, but they touched off a responsive chord in an American public eager to be stroked with compliments about their very own set of conquering demigods, and in the next two decades a stream of hero-books and treasuries, filled

126

Gib Morgan in the uniform of a Civil War veteran.

with pseudo-folklore and often catering to the juvenile market, would titillate and misinform American readers. As to his source for Kemp Morgan, Shay credits J. Frank Dobie and "my fellow members of the Texas Folk-Lore Society" with informing him of Kemp Morgan. The frontispiece and a chapter illustration of Kemp Morgan portray a Paul Bunyanesque figure, in keeping with the chapter's text, which begins, "A solitary man of gigantic proportions plodded wearily across the sandy plains of Eastern Texas."[105] The Chapter describes Morgan as a loner, "a complete oil gang all in one," who prospected by himself, sniffing for oil, drilled, built his own derrick, would cap and case the hole, and then turn the oil field over to a regular gang. Shay reported that oil drillers tell many stories of Kemp, such as the time his drill slowed down till it stopped, and he discovered he had drilled into an alum mine, which caused the hold to shrink around the drill; or the occasion he struck a rubber mine in Brazil and sold ten-foot lengths to a rubber manufacturer in Akron, Ohio; or how he pulled up duster (dry) holes, sawed them into four-foot lengths and sold them to Kansas farmers so they would not have to dig post holes in their hard soil. Shay introduced a cook, Bull Morrison, who told (in his own dialect) about the great derrick and the great bunkhouses that Kemp built and the greatest gusher in oil history, spouting up to heaven, that Kemp brought in.

Splotches of Shay's materials did resurface in Boatright's volume. The name Kemp is a misnomer, Gilbert being the legal first name and Gib the family nickname. Gib was never a strong giant, but he did create a giant tool dresser, Big Toolie, tall enough to grease the crown pulleys at the top of a derrick, but as Boatright says, Gib made Big Toolie a kind of good-natured moron and did little with him. Clearly Shay cast Morgan into Paul Bunyan dimensions, perhaps coalescing him with Big Toolie, but also incorporating the Munchausen element. Boatright's Gib Morgan does tell of drilling into alum and rubber, of constructing a sky-high derrick that had to be hinged in two places to let the moon pass by, and of various oilfield inventions with Rube Goldberg gimmickry. So Shay's slight chapter does nibble at the genuine oral tradition which must have brushed the members of the Texas Folklore Society by 1930. Some converging of Paul Bunyan and Gib Morgan tales did take place in the oil fields, with the lumberjack hero absorbing the exploits of his lesser known contemporary. Shay's insertion of Bull Morrison may have derived from Bunyan's associates.

Meanwhile other vendors of American pseudo-folk heroes borrowed from Shay and placed Kemp Morgan in their albums. In *The Hurricane's Children* (1937), Carl Carmer relates "How Kemp Morgan Greased the Sky"; and in *Yankee Doodle's Cousins* (1941) Anne Malcolmson devotes a section to Morgan. Furthermore Malcolmson retains the character of Bull Cook Morrison, who does not turn up in any of Gib's tales.

With the appearance of *Gib Morgan, Minstrel of the Oil Fields*, the facts and repertoire of Gib came into full view. We learn that Gilbert was born July 14, 1842, in Callensburg, Clarion County, in western Pennsylvania, less than eighteen years before the birth of the oil industry. His parents, also Pennsylvania born, had moved with him to Emlenton, less than forty miles from Titusville, Pennsylvania, where on August 28, 1859, a driller struck oil. The Civil War absorbed Gib's energies for the next several years, and from 1861 to 1864 he served in the Tenth Pennsylvania Reserve Infantry, and became known as the best storyteller in the regiment. Presumably these tall tales dealt with hunting, fishing, and farming, but would be eclipsed by his oilfield narrations. He is described at twenty-two as five feet nine and a half inches, one hundred and fifty pounds, dark-haired, with lively grey eyes and clean features. A photograph taken in his later years reveals a bushy mustache, prominent ears, and mousy face, rather belying the exploits he claimed. He promptly entered the oil industry swirling about his home territory and worked up to the position of oil well driller, the most skilled technician in the oil fields. Gib married in 1868, but his wife died four years later after the birth of their third son, and for the next twenty years Gib lived the life of a boomer, following the oil booms wherever they led him. His biographer lists Texas, Oklahoma, Kansas, West Virginia, and Pennsylvania as states where his comic tales are known, but Gib also worked in Indiana and Ohio. I recorded half a dozen of his tales in Michigan from the Texas-born wife of a student of mine. Boatright also states that Gib's name and legend have been carried to Mexico, Venezuela, Russia, and the East Indies by American oil crews. Yet he himself never worked in Texas. From 1894 until his death on February 19, 1909, Gib lived chiefly in old soldiers' homes in Indiana, Illinois, and finally in Tennessee. He was awarded a Civil War pension in 1897. Since the demands on an oil driller are rigorous, the twenty-eight active years that Gib spent in that capacity indicate his capabilities.

Throughout his life Gib enjoyed celebrity as a storyteller. One oil producer writing on "The Driller as I Knew Him," opined that but for his fondness for liquor Morgan might have achieved a reputation equal to Artemus Ward, Bill Nye or Mark Twain.[106] How addicted to drink Gib was remains a question, but the barroom was a favorite site for his yarnspinning. Observers comment that Gib would hang around saloons waiting for oil workers and producers to buy him drinks in exchange for his tales, which he would seemingly improvise on the moment. Several instances document his readiness to adapt a tale to a particular circumstance. In response to a pipeline worker who was ragging Gib about the low caliber of drillers, Gib related an episode he had experienced with shiftless pipeliners who had not saved enough money to return home from Ohio, so he offered to pipe them back, but by mistake he sent them feet first, and when they reached a Y, the right foot went to West Virginia and the left foot to Pennsylvania. "And that's the reason," concluded Gib, "there're so many half-men in the pipeline business."[107] Thus did Gib best his adversary, with a tale he customarily told to explain the demise of Big Toolie. Persons who heard Gib narrate remarked how he never told a tale the same way twice, and made an oft repeated yarn seem like one freshly minted. When a bullying foreman declared he had once killed a lazy workman, Gib launched into his narrative of an underwater fight with a black ditch digger on the bottom of the Ohio River, an uncharacteristic theme for peace-loving Gib, but effective in silencing the braggart. One attractive lie Gib used in bars to rustle drinks for himself was printed by Harry Botsford in the *Saturday Evening Post* for October 3, 1942, and heard by Boatright. This tale dealt with his attempt to curb the whickles, a cross between a canary and a bumblebee who loved crude petroleum and were drinking dry the wells of Pennsylvania. The only thing they liked better than crude oil was applejack, which Gib was sprinkling on bushes around oil wells to get them drunk so he could catch them. But applejack cost money, and Gib had little, so the oilfield workers understood Gib was trying to save their industry and pitched in. Botsford heard a different ending, that Gib had gone to Harrisburg to ask the governor to put a bounty on whickle scalps.[108]

Unfortunately the whickles story is the only example Boatright gives us of variant forms, and even then he does not supply literal texts. The value of his major contribution to American Folklore is vitiated by his failure to appreciate the necessity for exact texts, informant data, and comparative notes. His flawed work thus suffers by contrast with the scrupulous care on these matters given by Jansen in his study of Abe Smith and Lunt in his study of Jones Tracy. We cannot know which of the fifty-one texts ascribed to Gib are the most popular, or what was Gib's characteristic narrative style, as distinct from styles of those who retold his fictions, or how much editorial matter—for instance, in connections supplied be-

tween tales to give a sense of continuity—was supplied by Boatright. He bluntly states in his Preface:

> I have not attempted to set down the tales verbatim as they
> were told to me. This would have necessitated the printing of
> each tale in several versions, would have made the book less
> interesting, and would have served no useful purpose.

We can only shed tears at this statement so thoroughly wrong in
every aspect. The faithful reproduction of the oral tale is the first
law of the folklorist, the variants are of the greatest interest, and
the purpose served is, or should be, the aim of every practicing
folklorist, to capture, examine, and evaluate oral traditions as a
part of our cultural heritage. Tamper with the oral texts, and we do
not know what we are examining.

Still we must work with what we have and appreciate the cycles
of Hathaway Jones and Gib Morgan even if they are not in their
exact oral forms. The inventive imagination displayed by Gib Morgan in his oral narratives is unrivalled in American tall-tale folklore. But the esoteric references to oilfield technology in the
majority of the tales—37 out of 51—limits the audience and the
bearers of his tradition largely to participants in the oil industry.

The Repertoire: Gib outside the Oil Fields

Although primarily the oil driller, Gib in his tales did play other
roles, as farmer, fisherman, hunter, horseman, and businessman,
and these yarns show close links with the repertoires of other American Munchausens. Gib appropriates to his own saga extraordinary
animals that properly accompany a hero: the split hunting dog,
patched together with right legs up and left legs down that runs
faster than ever; the dog running alongside the train and cooling off
the hot box by urinating; the remarkable cow that produced ten
gallons of milk a day without milking after Gib shot her with
twenty quarts of nitroglycerin (a technique he learned from prod-
ding sluggish oil wells); the remarkable horse, Torpedo, weighing
twenty tons and twenty-two yards long, whom Gib simply threw
into reverse instead of turning around.[109] Gib also possessed remarkable guns: a rifle with a telescopic sight which he used to shoot
wild pigs in Texas at thirty miles range, so that he had to salt his

bullets to keep the meat from spoiling before he arrived; and a twenty-four barrel shotgun with which he shot a flock of pigeons that darkened the sun and buried him in birds seventy-two feet deep and three feet into the hardpan. As a fisherman he went after a big catfish in the lower Mississippi with a pine for a pole, a spool of drilling cable for a line, a steamboat anchor for a hook, and a steer for bait, and when he tossed the catfish onto the bank the river level fell two feet. These lies fall into the conventional categories of the great hunter and great fisherman, although Gib's mendacity seems audacious even for his ilk.

One narrative, "Gib's Boarding House," matches Paul Bunyan's giant cook shanty and offers a close variant of the great pancake griddle, one of the few traditional items in Bunyan lore. Gib built a monster plant in West Virginia to make buckwheat pancakes to serve in a boarding house he put up to accommodate oilfield workers. A dozen concrete mixers turned by steam engines churned the ingredients, and the batter was piped from a mile away into the kitchen onto the griddles, made from the bottoms of 43,000 barrel oil tanks heated by a gas well underneath. To grease the griddles he hired seven Negroes to skate over them on sides of fat bacon strapped to their feet. Gib served twenty-five thousand oilfield workers at a time.

A kindred fiction about a remarkable hotel Gib constructed moves away from tradition to creation.

GIB'S HOTEL

But after Spindletop came in and Gib came to Texas and saw the thousands of people that were crowding Beaumont without any place to stay, he decided he would put up a hotel for the general public. The building was forty stories high with ten high-speed elevators to bring the people up and down. When they stepped out of the elevator, no matter which floor, there was a narrow gauge railroad with a train waiting to take them to their rooms. In each room was a number of taps—one for ice water, one for Bourbon, one for rye, and one for Scotch, one for Tom Collins, one for old fashioned, and so on.

But the most remarkable thing about the hotel was its adaptation to the climate. Gib had noticed that throughout Texas and Oklahoma when a guest came in, he always asked for a south or east room. He never wanted a north or west room. So Gib built his hotel without any north or west rooms. Every guest who registered would be assigned to a south or east room. This would go on until all the rooms were filled. Every guest would go to bed in a room with a south or east exposure. But when those who had gone to bed first would wake up in the morning, they would look out through north or west windows and see the railroad tracks.

Gib's hotel was mounted on a turntable, but by the time his guests found it out, they were so pleased with the service, especially the spigot service, that they didn't mind.[110]

Instant liquor in the room and sun in the morning—Gib knew what visitors wanted, and he put his ingenuity to work. Save for the super hotel, Gib's tales (unconnected or only marginally connected with the oil industry) do not distinguish him from other Munchausens. The half dozen Gib lies I recorded in Michigan are standard tale types. Gib apparently never used his Civil War experience as a backdrop for personal exaggerations, nor have Civil War tall tales surfaced as a storytelling theme.

The Repertoire: Gib in the Oil Fields

Having cut his eye teeth on American stock windies of hunting, fishing, and farming, Gib turned his oral narrative powers to his lifelong occupation. As Boatright documents the point, both in his book about Gib and his later excellent study, *Folklore of the Oil Industry* (1963), the true wonders of the oil business—lucky strikes, heartbreaking misses, sudden fortunes, hoaxes, swindles, boom towns—made Gib's inflated yarns seem not so fantastic. Moreover, Gib's flair for technological details also helped lend an air of plausibility to his fancies.

Two of Gib's oilfield tall tales are familiar American lies which he grafted onto his scene: "Shingling on the Fog" and "Clinching the Mosquito Bills inside the Kettle." Gib's men lay shingles on the bandwheel house into the thick fog, before the sun comes out, and they come crashing down to earth; in the jungle they hide from mosquitoes under an oil tank, then brad the bills of the mosquitoes as they ram through it, until the mosquitoes fly off with the tank. For whatever reason, these are two of the most popular American lies; Jones Tracy, for example, tells both of them. But otherwise Gib's experiences drilling for oil seem original. His creation of Big

Toolie, who appears in four tales (two only briefly), and Strickie, the boa constrictor he annexed to his work crew and who helped out in six episodes, contributed some continuity and fraternity to Gib's adventures. Gib apparently did not do much with Big Toolie once he arrived with a new crew, "twenty-eight inches between the eyes and so tall that he could grease the crown pulleys without taking a foot off the ground." The big fellow played little tricks, such as putting his foot on the walking beam to stall the engine or throw the belt off; so one day Gib let the engine rip and the beam threw Big Toolie over the derrick and into the slush pit, whereupon he held out his hand, saying, "Mr. Morgan, I'm your man from now on."[111] But Big Toolie did little thereafter and met his end being piped from the islands back to the United States feet first and separating when he hit a Y at St. Louis. Strickie, however, played a real part in Gib's overseas undertakings.

The string of haps and mishaps involving the reptile began when Gib's company, Standard Oil of New Jersey, dispatched him to South America to drill for oil. They instructed him not to drill beyond ten thousand feet and only supplied him with ten thousand feet of cable, but Gib felt the signs looked promising and asked to continue.

HOW GIB DISCOVERED STRICKIE

While Gib was thinking and studying he started walking around, and pretty soon he was out in the jungle. And as he walked along thinking and studying, he came upon a big boa constrictor, a monstrous reptile, twenty blocks long if he was one. The snake had just swallowed a lot of monkeys, Gib figured, for there was a monkey's tail sticking out of his mouth, and he was lying there in a deep stupor not knowing Gib was anywhere about.

Gib went back and got the crew and they dragged the snake back to the rig, spiked his head to a spoke in the bull wheel, wound him around the shaft, and spliced his tail to the cable. In a few minutes they were cutting ditch again. The snake made as good a drilling cable as you ever saw—a lot better than this new steel cable—with just enough give to make the tools handle easy. Everything went fine for an hour or two. Then the jarring woke the snake up and he began wiggling. The next thing Gib knew he had worked the spike loose and was running off with the whole string of tools. He made for the jungle and got away before Gib could stop him.

Gib hired a bunch of Indians to help him track the snake down. They trailed him for two weeks and finally found him five hundred miles from the rig. He had dragged the tools around so much that the drill stem was worn down to the size of a crowbar.

How Strickie Bailed Out

Fortunately Gib had brought along another set of tools. He got to thinking about the way he had treated the big snake and he was downright ashamed of himself. He had found him sleeping peacefully and had dragged him off and driven a spike in his head and treated him rough. It was always better to be kind to dumb brutes.

So when Gib brought him back this time, he tried to win his friendship with kindness. First he went to the whisky well and got a barrel of whisky and gave it to him. When the snake had swallowed it, he began to wag his tail so friendly-like that Gib felt a deep affection for him. He named him Strickie, and every three weeks he fed him two hundred monkeys. He quit running at night so Strickie could have a rest, and each night when he shut down and unwound Strickie from the bull shaft, he gave him a barrel of whisky before he put him to bed. Strickie slept in front of Gib's bunkhouse door, and he wouldn't let man or beast come near until Gib ordered him down. It was not long until Strickie was the most valuable piece of equipment Gib had.

After Gib started drilling again and had let out about twenty feet of snake, he pulled the tools to bail out the cuttings. Then he realized how absent minded he had been. The sand line wasn't any longer than the drilling cable. If one wouldn't reach the bottom, the other wouldn't either. So the only thing he knew to do was to unwind Strickie and put him on the sand line. Gib was getting ready to tie his head to the line and his tail to the bucket, but Strickie kept changing ends on him. At first Gib thought he was just being playful. But from the way he kept wagging his tail and sticking it up against the end of the rope Gib saw that he wanted him to tie them together. Gib couldn't see that it made any difference, and so if Strickie preferred to go down head first, he was willing to let him.

As soon as Gib got the splice made, Strickie darted into the well and began to unwind the sand reel before Gib could stop him to tie on the bailer. He let him down to the bottom of the well and reeled him out. Strickie crawled to the sand pit and began to disgorge pumpings. From that time on Gib never used the bailer. Strickie had a bigger capacity and could clean the well with one lowering.

How Gib Recovered His Tools

After Gib had been using Strickie about two weeks, the cable bootjacked off just above the rope socket. Gib let down a horn socket and caught the tools all right, but as he was trying to pull them out the latch in the socket broke and he lost them. And there he was with a string of tools in the well and no way to get them out.

He had his tool dresser fire up the forge and they went to work trying to make a new latch. While they were working, Strickie began wiggling so that he stook the whole rig. Gib realized that there wan't any use in leaving him all wound up with the cable while they worked maybe the whole day on the horn socket. So he unwound him and gave him his whisky. As soon as he had swallowed it, Strickie crawled up on the derrick floor to the casing head and stuck his head in the well and began wagging his tail. Then Gib caught on to what was in his mind all along. He tied his tail to the cable and let him down. When he drew him up the tools came with him. Strickie had swallowed the rope socket, the sinker, the jars, and half the drill stem. Gib drilled a lot of wells after that and used a lot of newfangled equipment, but he never had a better fishing tool than Strickie.

More Cable

The well went along fine. Gib hadn't found oil, but indications looked better and better every day. Gib's only worry was that Strickie might not be long enough to reach the oil he knew was down there. Each day there would be a little more of Strickie in the well and a little less on the bull wheels. When he shut down one Saturday night there was just enough of Strickie left to wrap once around the shaft. Gib had got a showing of oil that day, and he knew that he was right on top of something big and he stayed awake all night worrying about how to get to it.

But the next morning all his worries were over. That very night Strickie shed his skin and Gib had plenty of cable to finish the well.

Strickie Delivers Again

It was a gusher, But Gib closed it in and soon had it running into the storage. In no time at all it had filled the one thirty-thousand-barrel storage tank the mosquitoes had left. Gib shut it in and began laying a gathering line to the coast, where the big new tanker steamers that Standard had just put on could

load. His pipe ran out when he was still about half a mile from
the harbor, but by that time Strickie had shed again and his skin
not only finished out the line but left enough over to reach up on
deck and fill the compartments without all the bother of making
pipe connections.

STRICKIE'S LAST DAYS

Gib kept Strickie with him for years after that, and when Gib
retired, Strickie retired too. The company gave him a pension
and he lived in the Bronx, where he would have plenty of company. He still got his barrel of whisky every night and his two
hundred monkeys every three weeks. Gib never came to New
York without dropping by to see him.[112]

We have to imagine Gib reciting the saga of Strickie as a series of
personal incidents or perhaps one continuous chronicle. Once the
idea seized him of substituting the reptile for the drilling cable he
played with further possibilities: the snake could clean the cuttings
at the well's bottom; he could retrieve lost tools that had fallen down
the well; he could shed his skin to supply more cable. Having played
out the fancy, Gib retired Strickie to the Bronx. The hero's faithful
and marvelous animal companion is a standard figure in mythic
narratives, usually a horse or dog, and Gib here has contrived an
occupational animal helper in place of a warrior's beast friends. No
parallel to Strickie can be found in American folklore, of an intelli-
gent creature serving the master hero, save possibly Paul Bunyan's
Babe the Blue Ox, who represents bulk rather than sagacity, and
belongs more to literary than to folk tradition.

Another original theme that Gib pursued with obvious relish concerned unusual substances he encountered when drilling for oil. In
his various operations in the Fiji Islands and South America he
struck bay run, quinine, whiskey, rubber, buttermilk, champagne,
sweet cream, and alum, and failed to locate essence of peppermint.
Encountering these unexpected liquids compelled him to take un-
anticipated actions. Drilling into sweet cream gave him the idea of
manufacturing ice cream and selling it to the heathens, but by the
time he had returned to the States to purchase and bring back an
ice cream factory, the cream had turned sour, and he lost a fortune.
When he struck a gusher of clear, sweet-smelling bay rum and filled
a two thousand barrel tank with it, his production bosses told him

to drill one more screw, and he drilled through the bay rum field into "an unmentionable liquid that brought back memories of his boyhood days when he worked in a livery stable." Once in the Fiji Islands when Gib left his crew for a week to accept an invitation from the Noble, Grant, Worshipful Master, Chancellor, Commander, Exalted Ruler and Jobbonaney, they drilled into champagne sand, and on his return he found them so drunk he could never get them back to work again and had to abandon them on the island. Down in South America Gib struck rubber, causing the tools to bounce back up the well higher each time, and up into the derrick, until they knocked off the crown block. Gib waited until the rubber had been penetrated and then had his tool dresser catch the sinker, repair the crown block, reattach the cable, and resume drilling. But at another rubber well the vein was not thick enough to throw the tools high enough for the tools to drill through, and Gib had to abandon the hole; twenty years later the tools—tons of steel—were said to be still bouncing, day and night and Sundays.

As with other American Munchausens, Gib's known repertoire does not include off-color stories or sexual exploits. The closest reference to an indecency occurs when he told about how he drilled on Pike's Peak and rode a mule to cover the steep incline from the engine to the rig. Riding the mule down the mountain, he saw the mule's head between the stirrups, then felt something warm on the back of his neck. He felt under his overcoat collar and his hand did not smell like cologne. Thereafter he threw a saddle on the belt that ran from the rig to the engine and rode that way. In a letter published in 1900 in S. W. Munn's *Useful Information for Oil Men* (in which he wrote down some of his stories, with deliberate misspellings and mispunctuation), Gib gives this tale saying he "raked out about a half peck of mulc dung" from under his overcoat collar.[113] Whether Professor Boatright or his informant adjusted this reference, or Gib himself for his written version, we cannot be sure. We do know that the Munchausen of the Oilfields avoided scatology and relied on his powers of comic invention and intimate knowledge of drilling processes to create his own legend.

FIVE

Len Henry

(1852–1946)

THE Munchausen hero bobbed up in northern Idaho in the person of Len Henry, prairie farmer, stock raiser, one-time gold digger in California, freighter in Oregon, wild horse breeder in eastern Washington, and the last of the pioneer squawmen on the Nez Perce reservation at Lapwai, Idaho, where he died on March 14, 1946. He claimed to have been born December 30, 1841, at Kansas City, Kansas, which would have made him 104 at the time of his death, but people reportedly said of this allegation: "That's the last lie old Len Henry will ever tell." Through his Indian wife he received a government allotment when the Nez Perce reservation was opened near the tiny village of Sweetwater, Idaho, and he removed there about 1889. A photograph taken of him shortly before he died shows a sturdy old màn belying his years, hair over his ears under an upturned hat, hands on hips, in floppy trousers, gazing firmly at the camera in front of his cabin.

In the absence of white women, early pioneers in the Idaho territory began taking Indian wives as early as 1846, a practice that led to their being dubbed "squawmen." These wives cooked meals, washed dishes and clothes, cut firewood, milked the cows and fed the pigs, and provided a cheerful homecoming for the homesteaders, who in their bachelor days would return tired and hungry to a cold cabin stacked high with dirty dishes. Len Henry's brother Noble ("Nobe") recalled how he wed an Indian woman:

> "I came to Idaho in 1863 at the age of 18, following a packtrain and freighting for several years, finally homesteading on Asotin Creek. After batching three years, I noticed that two of my neighbors with Indian wives were getting along much better than I.
>
> "One day I mentioned to one of the Indian wives that I needed help. In no time at all she had three Indian women at her home for me to choose from."[114]

Noble prospered so well that Len followed suit, and a tale grew that he picked his wife out of a female line-up.

Four of Len Henry's stories were published the year after his death by Robert G. Bailey in *River of No Return,* namely the Great Salmon River of Idaho. Bailey, the Nez Perce County Historian for the Idaho State Historical Society, subtitled his book "A Century of Central Idaho and Eastern Washington History and Development." Len Henry lived during this period, which linked the old lurid West of the early sixties and prosaic West of the present. The tales and brief preface to them printed by Bailey carry special interest as a direct report from an observer of Len Henry and are reproduced below:

"TRUE" STORIES OF LEN HENRY

Len Henry, whose death is recorded earlier in this volume, was an inveterate story teller. His were always "true" stories, and he was invariably the hero. Whenever he was in a reminiscent mood, which was when he could get a bunch of listeners together, he could ramble on seemingly without end. Just as a sample of the many thousands of tales he told his cronies, the following four come to mind:

"That reminds me of the time I was doing scout duty for the army. I was sent up in an observation balloon. I had finished my observations and a favorable wind was drifting me back towards our lines. Just then a guest of wind titled the balloon and I was thrown out. I landed squarely in the center of a paved road. The force of the fall was so great that both feet were driven into the paving up to my hips. I had a little difficulty extricating myself, but eventually did so and made my report in time for the army to advance and score a signal victory.

"One day when I was in the mountains riding horseback, I came to a place where there was a slide of moving rock fully 12 feet wide. It was impossible for my horse to cross it. I took out my lash rope (lariat) and swung the loop toward a stump on the other side of the slide. I made a good throw, and the loop settled snugly around the stump. I tied the end to the horn of the saddle, turned my horse at right angles down the hill, and dug the spurs into his flanks. He gave a tremendous leap into the air, and when the rope tightened sailed clear to the other side of the slide.

"Once when I was down on the Salmon River I had occasion to make a crossing. Having no boat or other method of getting to the other side, I went up to a high bluff and jumped. I was just about to land safely, when, glancing down at the sandy beach, I saw a large rattlesnake coiled up below me. Without stopping to think or reason, I just naturally turned an about-face in the air and returned to the spot I had just left when I started to jump.

"One day when I was in the mountains with a pack train, I came to a steep trail which was exceptionally full of abrupt turns. I had a little dog with me. After a time, looking back the dog was nowhere in sight. Tying up my horse I went back to investigate. I found the dog stuck at one of the switchbacks. In attempting to make the turn, it was so acute that he had doubled himself into a right-angle knot and could go neither forward nor backward."[115]

As Bailey indicates, Len loved to yarn and to make himself the hero of his escapades. All four of these texts present Len as the narrator, where almost all of Len's tales subsequently collected refer to him in the third person, the natural tendency as distance lengthens between the Munchausen and his retellers. The first narrative contains the popular motif of the strong hero who sinks into solid rock or concrete, customarily when carrying a heavy burden, but Henry prefers to fall from a great height during army maneuvers. The second displays Len in his favorite role, as extraordinary horseman and roper performing a daredevil deed. In some variants he enhances this adventure by making it an escape from the Indians. The third again embodies a familiar exaggeration Munchausens like to adopt, the jumper who for some danger or because he believes the distance is too great reverses himself in midflight. Finally Len relates an unusual episode, not reported for other fabulists but recurrent with variant touches in his cycle, the dog-stuck-on-crooked-trail. Sometimes instead of a pack train Len drives a freight wagon drawn by mules or horses; while Bailey's version leaves the dog in his dilemma, other accounts give Len credit for extricating him by snapping the dog by the tail to straighten him out, but for the twenty-four years that he lived thereafter, the dog suffered from a kink in its back.[116]

The extent of Len Henry's storytelling fame did not become apparent until the 1960s, when folklorist Jan Brunvand, then on the faculty of the University of Idaho, set on the trail of the Idaho Munchausen. By then nothing about Len remained in print. Brunvand collected, corresponded, and encouraged his students to collect, and amassed 67 separate tales, with 116 variants from 23 tellers.[117] These he classified into 19 tales well known in American tall-tale lore: the submerged watch found still running long after; the horse tied to the church steeple; the snake-bit hoe handle that swells; the planted buggy whip that sprouts. Another 18 made use of general motifs but imparted original twists to them: Len cavorts as a remarkable rider, roper, blacksmith, thresher, and spitter, and glorifies his own legend. In such long bows he related how he once rode fast enough to overtake and bulldog a deer and another time rode an elk to escape from Indians. Another 17 tales seemed to be unique, such as the dog caught in the crooked trail, or Len's account of saving Custer's army and killing the squaw who scalped Custer. Len even concocted a jocular personal narrative about a cherished Nez Perce belief: he said that he had fasted in the mountains and waited for a guardian spirit, which finally appeared as a big gray wolf, whereupon Len asked the animal to wait for him while he went back and had lunch. The solitary fasting vigil while awaiting the tutelary guardian represents a solemn pan-Indian ritual, but the Nez Perce relished and retold Len's spoof. Finally, 13 anecdotes circulated about Len and his brother Nobe, probably fanned by Len himself. In one such story Len sold three ganders to a man who wished to raise geese. In some four-fifths of all his narratives Len talked about his own derring-do.

Besides the texts of these lies Brunvand also obtained information on Len's storytelling style and reputation. In the 1960s, folks in Washington, Montana, and Idaho recollected how Len (sitting cross-legged on the floor of a grocery story chewing tobacco) would entertain fifteen to twenty men from morning to night, slowing down only to wipe the chewing tobacco from his chin, and finally get up without touching his hands to the floor. One of Len's admirers remembered walking four miles to hear his stories. Len also yarned around campfires on hunting or freighting trips through the mountains and in Indian sweathouses. An older woman, who as a child had known Len, wrote Brunvand: "We considered him very famous as our father always repeated the stories he heard, and we had many a good laugh in the evenings at home. Mr. Henry was . . . very droll and slow of motion and speech. He . . . would listen to the other men spin yarns, then he could always tell one better."[118] In social or business situations Len would slip casually into a lie, and listeners trying to draw him out could not be sure whether he was fabricating or not. A good example of his deceptive manner is recalled by Barney McGovern, who related ten Len Henry tales to Brunvand:

GRASSHOPPERS IN WINTER

One time there was a fellow came there to our place to buy a cow. And Len was up. You see the original place was up on Asotin Creek [eastern Washington]; Nobe had a place up there. And he was tellin' about one time he pulled in there and he said they wanted some fish. "Well," he says, "in the fall of the year—fish hadn't gone down yet, so" he said, "there was about six or eight inches of snow on the ground. "Well," he says, "I just went and kicked around and I got a couple dozen grasshoppers, and I went out," he says, "and I used them grasshoppers, and in no time," he says, "why I had ten-twelve fish in just a few minutes. And I went back, kicked around, and I got another dozen or fifteen grasshoppers . . ." Just about that time he happened to think, you know, that grasshoppers when snow's on, there's no such a thing, you know. He says, "That was the damndest year for grasshoppers *I* ever seen."[119]

Lies about mixed weather are popular all over the United States, not surprisingly considering the abrupt changes that occur in actuality, and the way the population fastens onto weather reports. (In Rhode Island "Shepherd Tom" Hazard in his book of folklore ramblings, *The Johnny-Cake Letters,* recalled a fellow thrown into a snowbank who was helped out by grassmowers.) Len Henry weaves the fiction into his role as the great fisherman, which blends with his other roles as the great hunter, the great horseman, and the great roper.

SIX

Jones Tracy

(1856–1939)

*O*N Mount Desert Island off the southern Maine coast, known to summer visitors from New York for the resort town of Bar Harbor, a teller of hunting stories and tall tales gained a local reputation that made him into a modest folk hero. In 1863, at the age of seven, Jones Tracy moved to Mount Desert (from Harrington on the mainland), when his father bought a good-sized farm on the island; and there Jones lived his long life. In addition to farming he built stone walls, shored up wells, served as game warden, and managed a dance hall and rooming house attached to farm property he acquired in 1914 on his sister's death. Much of his reputation as a storyteller emerged during his running of the dance hall, which catered to nearby quarry workers and the local residents.

A trained folklorist, C. Richard K. Lunt, who obtained his doctorate in folklore at Indiana University and himself resided on Mount Desert Island, published in 1969 an excellent seventy-four page study and collection of *Jones Tracy, Tall-Tale Hero from Mount Desert Island.*[120] This model monograph contains 53 annotated texts of tales associated with Tracy, recorded in 1963 and 1964 by Lunt from thirteen informants (several of them also tellers of repute), along with biographical and analytic chapters considering Tracy as a raconteur of exaggerative humor and as a folk hero. A valuable appendix provides sketches of the interview sessions and the informants.

144

Jones Tracy

The front cover reproduces a photograph of Jones Tracy with a gun in his left hand and a pole on his right shoulder from which hangs a string of dead rabbits. He is wearing overalls, hip boots, sweater, and porkpie hat, and appears of sturdy build, not more than five feet seven inches, with smooth features, close-set eyes and a drooping mustache. The photograph in no way suggests a humorist but a serious huntsman, framed against lofty fir trees.

From where did Jones Tracy get his tall stories and his penchant for dispensing them? Family saga may have stimulated him, as one ancestor, Caleb Tracy, was supposed to have thrashed British soldiers in the Revolution and thrown a twelve hundred pound horse over a fence. On hunting trips he would swap yarns with companions in overnight cabins. The society in which he grew up, of woodsmen, farmers, game wardens, peddlers, was peopled with characters and tale tellers, and storytelling formed an important part of their leisure pursuits. Jones Tracy found an unexpected audience among the weekly dance hall visitors who attended from all over the island

and spilled over into his kitchen to hear him yarn. As his reputation grew, he was always in demand, at the store or in the post office, to tell his latest story. A son-in-law recalls special qualities of Jones's style. "And I never heard anyone else tell it that way. . . . He'd be in a green grove for a while, and then he'd be on a hardwood ridge. And you's right alongside of him all the time. And then you'd wind up, *out of this world!*"[121] So did Jones lead his listeners up the garden path with verisimilitude only to end in fantasyland.

Jone's repertoire falls into long deer-hunting stories based on his actual experiences and shorter tall tales found in general circulation. Lunt also collected, as have other folklorists on the trail of Munchausens, anecdotes about Jones' wit and "cleverality," in which he becomes the subject of comic legendry. Davy Crockett likewise told realistic bear-hunting stories and stock tall tales and became the subject of trickster anecdotes. A son-in-law and a grandson of Jones estimate his reservoir of deer-hunting rigmaroles at three to four hundred and considered them his primary narratives, related more seriously than the others, but relatively few have endured, because of their length and individual quality. Lunt recorded 19 tall tales in 54 multiple versions, 23 tall tales in only one version, and 11 anecdotes, one with three variants, told by and usually about Jones Tracy. Of this batch, only one represents the longer deer-hunting personal vein, and Lunt singles it out for special consideration.[122] A son of Jones, Ralph Tracy, sixty, who had worked for both the John D. Rockefeller and Nelson Rockefeller estates on the island, and knew well his father's repertoire and style, recapitulated this yarn. It describes a hunt in winter in which Jones displayed considerably more smarts about deer-tracking than his friendly rival, Orvil, even though the hunt took place on Orvil's turf. Replete with dialogue and personal references, the story would appeal only to a limited local audience, familiar with deer hunting techniques and the personalities involved. At the time Lunt prepared his study the term "personal experience narrative" had not come into use by folklorists, but this is the genre into which falls the tale "Jones and Orvil Hunt Deer," and presumably the several hundred unrecovered similar deer hunt yarns. Other narratives collected by Lunt deal with deer hunts, but they all fall under the genre of tall tales collected elsewhere. A good example is "The Bunghole Story," reported in four variants, three in brief anecdotal style but one in the extended, detailed manner associated with Jones Tracy's personal experience narratives. The teller, John Carroll, 88, was a son-in-law of Jones.

THE BUNGHOLE STORY

This happened over here on Sargent's mountain. The most of his deer stories were on Sargent's mountain. Well, what made them interesting, he'd tell about what time he started: generally started before daylight early in the morning. This morning he got up early and milked his cows and fed his stock. And it was the first [frost]. There wasn't any storms, but he said the trees was covered with frost. You've seen these mornings with the bushes all white with frost. When the sun comes up it soon melts it and runs off. And he said it was dark when he left the old Tracy house up there. And he went right down across the road you know, over on Sargent's mountain. That was his hunting ground. And he got up the mountain, and of course he went slow after he got down on his hunting ground. And he was looking and peeking and creeping along through the woods, and he said it was, he judged it was about eleven o'clock before he got up there; then settled down the mountain and looking and creeping as easy as he could and he sighted this buck deer not far from him. And he up with his gun and took good aim, and he said he had plenty of time. Took good aim with his rifle, and fired.

And he hit him on the side of the head. Knocked one horn off, and I think it almost hit his brain, but not quite, and it numbed him. He fell down when it knocked his horn off. He dropped right in his tracks just the same as you'd hit him with a hammer. And Jones he said he started along there and when he got up to him, he said he stood his gun up side of a tree there and went along and pulled his knife out to bleed him, you know. And just as he reached out to bleed him, to jiggle him, the deer opened his eyes and looked up at him and turned over and got up on his feet. And he said, "I made a grab for him like that," he says. "My big finger went through his bunghole and," he says, "I hooked him and of course he was towing me. It wasn't so hard for me as it was for the deer." And he said he run along there. He described the road down to the south there for quite a while, right along the side of the mountain, and then he turned over on the other side. "Well," he said, "it was about eleven o'clock when I fired that shot, and before I gained on him enough to give him a slat, slat him off his feet down, it was about two hours and fifteen minutes." Just as tight as he could run before he could slat him off his feet and stick his knife in his neck.[123]

Customarily this lying tale is given in a sentence or two. In another telling, it is compressed into this one-sentence version:

> This one isn't fit to tell, but it was about the one when he chased the deer three miles before he stuck his finger in the deer, and he chased him three more miles before he could crook his finger over and stop the deer.[124]

Another teller did mention the "deer's rectum" as the point of insertion, but all three narrators of the short form approached the tale gingerly, as casting reflection on Jones or themselves. One even attributed its origin to Kit Carson, who was "quite a storyteller," and, having wounded a grizzly bear and run out of ammunition, reached into the bear's rear and ran miles with him before he could bend his finger. The story also gets attached to the cycle of John Darling, the Catskill Munchausen.[125]

By contrast with these brief texts, the elaborate recital by John Carroll conveys the scenic portraiture and details of deer tracking characteristic of Jones Tracy's style, especially as unfolded in personal narratives.

Rather than categorize Jones's stock by tall-tale variants and miscellaneous stories, I would divide it into (1) exaggerative accounts of his strength and skill, (2) extraordinary events and phenomena he had witnessed, and (3) anecdotes of eccentric characters in the vicinity. The first category, his forte, embraced both personal deeds and standard tall tales, such as "The Bunghole Story." Jones adapted many standard American lies of hunting and fishing, marksmanship and feats of stamina, and special skills with tools, to his own legend, and thus acquired local fame both as storyteller and as superman. Those tall tales he could not attach to his persona he related as an eyewitness. Also, in the American vein, he indulged in comic stories about the odd individuals who attract attention in every community. The life of outdoors, of farms and the woods and waters and open sky, permeates Jones's narratives. They deal not only with deer but foxes, bears, pigs, ducks, turkeys, trout, mosquitoes, snakes, and in the vegetable world, blueberries, carrots, apples, which may exhibit unusual features or serve as props for Jones's actions. Hunting, shooting, fishing, ploughing, planting form the backdrop for Jones's dramas.

Jones Tracy as Superhero

A number of tales celebrate Tracy's physical prowess. In bed on the verge of pneumonia, he grew restless and, in spite of the rain, grabbed his gun, crawled through Aunt Betty's Pond, shot five black ducks, and ran all the way home just in time for dinner, saying he never felt better. Aghast, the doctor told Jones he had broken the grippe by running and sweating, but if he had taken a chill it would have killed him. This exploit smacks of an inflated personal experience narrative. So do other occasions on which he lugged almost back to camp a deer he had shot but not dressed; defeated a rival logging crew in cutting timber by winding a five pound lead around a sharpened broad axe and felling trees with two strokes; made a punching bag out of cement and gravel placed in a meal bag, and knocked it right through the shed into the cook shack, tipping over the cook stove and starting a fire. Such yarns do not appear in the general canon of American whopperdom. But others do: for example, Tracy's picking up a plow he was pushing and pointing to himself when accosted by some fellows inquiring for Jones Tracy; or reaching down a bear's throat and turning him inside out, at the same time changing him from a black bear to a white one; or sinking into concrete or rock when carrying a sack of ammunition or being struck by a falling timber.

Tracy also spread tales about his shooting prowess. Versions of "The Wonderful Hunt,"[126] most enduring of all American exaggerations, turn up in Tracy's arsenal, in the forms of "The Split Bullet," "The Great Shot," and "The Curved Gun Barrel." Variants of each of these follow.

THE SPLIT BULLET

> Well, Jones went hunting, and in those days they was these wild turkeys. And he only had one bullet. And he said they was fifteen of them in the family, and he knew one turkey wouldn't be any good, so he'd have to weigh his shot to hit two turkeys anyway. So he run alongside of this brook, and he saw these two turkeys, one on each side of a rock.
>
> And old Jones said, "I aimed right for a point on that rock and split that bullet and killed both of those turkeys." And he said, "That gun kicked me so," he said, "that it kicked me over into the brook." And he said, "when I come up the seat of my pants

was so full of trout," he said, "that it burst off the suspender button and shot a partridge."[127]

Of the several forms of "The Wonderful Hunt," this is the American classic, doubtless a wish-fulfillment fantasy on the frontier, where the one shot would bring in such a mixed bounty of game. Another variation has the hunter with the single shot strike down a startling number of the same species.

THE GREAT SHOT

There was that sunken heath just in back of where he lived, and it used to be fabulous duck shooting there at one time. 'Course he told about the time he sneaked out along the edge of the bank, and these ducks were asleep. So he kept working around until he got them all lined up, and then he quacked once like a duck.

And when they stuck their heads up, he had just a rifle, so he shot all their heads off. Seven or eight birds.[128]

The original touch here, showing Jones's "cleverality" as well as his marksmanship, comes in the hunter's imitation of the duck. In another great-shot tale Jones shoots a buck, a doe, and a fawn with the one bullet.

A third family of one-bullet shots emanates from "The Bent Gun Barrel."

THE BENT GUN BARREL

Of course you've probably heard the one about the deer running around the mountain. Yes, he was going into Southwest Valley one morning and he saw this deer running around the mountain. He only had one bullet. So the deer jumped behind a tree. And he knew that he couldn't get a shot straight away so he bent the gun barrel and fired. He said the deer kept right on running, and he said the next week he was going in and he saw this deer about the same bigness, but . . . 'twas so thin, still running. And so he hollered "Whoa," he said. And when the deer stopped the bullet caught up with him and killed him.[129]

Again an original twist, the continuous flight of the beast halted by the hero's command, distinguishes a familiar lie. Another variant attached to Jones lacks these touches and has Jones bend a shotgun in the crotch of an apple tree to shoot a flock of birds in a ditch.

His shooting skills also were displayed on two occasions when he was out of shot. Once he transfixed a deer with a straightened fish hook, known as a mackerel jig, and pulled it in hand over hand like a mackerel. Another time he nailed the tail of a fox to a tree with shingle nails (or a ramrod); the fox ran right out of his skin, and Jones was three days catching him. Coupled with his shooting prowess was his running speed in the tale "Patting the Bullet Along." Having shot at a deer with his old 50–95 Sharps rifle, he would chase the slow bullet with a wooden paddle and pat it on course until it hit the deer.

The speed afoot again becomes evident in "Jones and the Presque Isle Race Trace," apparently another personalized narrative. Walking back from the Maine woods he came to the track on Presque Isle, and feeling the need for more exercise ran four times around the mile track, then had to run around twice more before he could slow down to get out the gate. Jones also acquired a fast horse, like the Heroic Age champions whose steeds matched their masters' powers. In an extended personal recitation, "Jones' Fast Horse," the hero recounts a trip he took to a neighbor's to get a peck of oats; whipping his horse with an alder, he "kept in sight of the sun for three days." This tale again illustrates Jones' characteristic style of narrating a perfectly reasonable and fully detailed piece that at the end erupts into the impossible.

Not only was Tracy strong and powerful, he was also ingenious, dexterous and resourceful, as another cluster of yarns bears witness. In perhaps his most celebrated achievement, "Riding the Spar" (recovered in five assorted variants), Tracy cut and limbed a spar on Brown's Mountain, then waited for a snowfall with a good crust and rode down on the spar, dressed in a swallowtail coat. One teller did not know why he was so dressed up, but another said he was going to a party and, taking a short cut over Brown's Mountain, jumped on a log to slide down. The spar-log gathered speed and struck a pine tree, splitting it in two; Tracy and the log sailed through; the tree closed behind and snapped off the coat tails; and "they're right there in that tree today." In one text he picked two pails of blueberries on the way down, but this motif appears to belong to a separate brag featuring the quantities of blueberries on Mount Desert Island's mountains and the speed of the hero in picking them from a ship tacking up the Sound. In another telling Tracy was caught in the tree by the coattails and had to wiggle free.[130]

In the John Darling cycle, the Catskill Mountain hero peeled half a big maple tree on top of a mountain and rode it five miles down to the other side to greet his wife for dinner, peeling the rest of the log en route. In a separate tale about Darling, but widely dispersed, seven yoke of oxen ran away while he was plowing new ground, the plow split a big oak stump, which closed up and caught him by the seat of the pants.[131] These two elements combine in Tracy's adventure.

In other bragging tales Tracy reveals further accomplishments. He whittled and painted wooden tolers, or duck decoys, in such lifelike manner that the cat ate off their heads when he left them to dry behind the stove overnight. As a cook one winter in northern Maine he cooked so many biscuits that the camp used the flour barrels for fire wood without other supply and had to employ a double team to haul away the sawdust. And in building a hunting camp he had no equals. His son Ralph Tracy relates the following tale.

How Jones Built a Camp

John Lynam was going to build a camp. Of course father already had a camp. John Lynam being a sportsman—hunting season in those days, you know—he wanted a sporting camp in the valley. And he wanted to know if my father knew how to build a camp. My father told him, "Yes, I believe I can build a camp. At least I built my own."

"Well," he said, "I want to know for sure if you can build a camp. I don't want none of these halfway jobs."

"Well," he said, "I built a few. I built my own."

He said, "How did you build your own? I want to know just how you're going to build me a camp."

"Well," he said, "the first thing I did," he said, "I want up on the side of Bubby Mountain," which they called it then, Bubble Mountain. "I cut two spar spruce and made twenty-two feet long, and I lopped off twelve inches at the top end. "Well," he said, "I took them on my shoulder," he said, "brought them down. I threw them down." And he said, "I took my narrow axe, my chopping axe," he said, "and I went in and got my long jointer," he said, "and come out." He said, "And I put that old plane on there so I took the shaving the whole length and never broke the shaving."

"Well," John said, "you can build a camp." He said, "I'll guarantee you can!"[132]

Known parallels do not exist for this text, which appears to be one of Tracy's personal compositions, based on his own knowledge of workmanship with wood. But the theme of the rustic native overturning the city slicker has a long history in American lore. This text well captures the dialogue exchange, reminiscent of the Arkansas Traveler, between the two folktypes. And as customary Tracy emerges with heroic powers.

Jones Tracy as Storyteller

In those instances where Tracy could not attach a tall tale to his own qualities, he at least enhanced his reputation for drawing the long bow by describing marvels he had observed. He spoke of pigs fed a special ration that diminished their size until they disappeared down rat holes; of carrots as large as his arm; of a man stuck in mud up to his waist, who told Tracy not to worry for he was standing on a hayrack; and other such old-timers. One of some originality depicts Tracy in a story-matching contest with a chap hanging around the store, who claimed that he had greatly improved the taste of the apples from a tree on his farm by putting old pieces of iron around the tree. Tracy claimed he'd had an apple tree so tasteless that even the hogs wouldn't eat the fruit. He drove half a dozen horseshoe nails into the tree, and the next year "she bore two armored cruisers and a battleship." The first chap took Tracy aside and asked, "Do you doubt my word?" "No," replied Tracy "do you doubt mine?"[133] Here we have Tracy's tale-of-a-tale-within-a-tale as recounted by his grandson, demonstrating Tracy's ability to defeat a competing fabulist.

Another set of anecdotes about Tracy, which he most likely fostered himself, portrays him as a quick-witted trickster outsmarting the law when caught poaching deer. Asked one spring day what the deer hairs on the sleeve of his mackinaw signified, he promptly replied that he had not worn it since hunting the previous fall. Tracy killed two deer on a Sunday morning, contrary to the law against hunting on Sunday, then told a game warden he had shot them the night before. The warden touched one animal and re-marked that it has hot; Tracy observed what a warm night it had been on Saturday! Having shot a moose out of season, Tracy flagged a stranger and offered him some of the meat to help him drag the creature out to the road. "Do you know who I am?" asked the man. "No." "I'm the new warden." Tracy asked him, "Do you know who I am?" "No." "I'm the biggest liar in the State of Maine." The last jest is again an American favorite. Such vignettes cast Tracy as the trickster-hero complementing his strong-man attributes.

A character himself, Tracy appreciated other characters whose sayings and doings set stories in motion, and two of his best yarns feature such personalities. One was a stuttering hunting companion of his, Frank Thompson, who became suddenly afflicted with a ter-rible cough when he and Tracy stopped at the doctor's at Bar Harbor to get some whiskey for Tracy's cold, during Prohibition times. Tracy spun out the tale with circumstantial touches and reproduced Frank's stuttering and wheezing. Here the character plays the de-ceiver. In another local character anecdote the protagonist, given four different names in four variants, plays the fool, in a narrative reported internationally. One text follows.

CARRYING THE BAG OF GRAIN

That was uncle Leonard. He walked over to Somesville, [to] Jack Whiting, or . . . whoever did keep the store at that time. He bought this bag of grain and started walking home. Somebody came along with a horse and wagon and [said], "Uncle Leonard, would you like a ride?" "He didn't care if he did" [imitation of voice of old man]. "Well," he said, "you go and jump in there back of those bags, cubby hole in the back of the wagon. You jump in there and have a ride." He got way down to Bordeau's, he said, "Uncle Leonard, aren't you going to lay that bag of grain down?"

"Oh no," he said, "the horse'll lug me. I'll hold the grain" [imi-tation of voice of old man].[134]

In the episodes in which he stars, in the reports about him, and in the memorable tales linked to his name, Jones Tracy achieved a Munchausen stature on Mount Desert Island.

Daniel Stamps

(1866–1950)

A long limestone ridge divides the Illinois and Mississippi rivers in Calhoun County, Illinois, to form an isolated, leisurely society given to fishing, farming, and yarning. There Dan'l Stamps idled his time and spun windies during much of his life, particularly around Kampsville. In Stamps' day Calhoun was the only Illinois county lacking railroad service, and even the roads were few, but Calhoun County grew over a million bushels of apples a year. A modest but suggestive article by Warren S. Walker, "Dan'l Stamps: Tall Tale Hero of the River Country," presents thirteen texts attributed to Stamps. Although Walker includes some synopses of variants and background information, he does not provide an analysis of narrative style or comparative notes and merely lists his twelve informants.[135]

Dan'l Stamps emerges as a figure of legend talked about in Calhoun, Greene, and Jersey counties. Exploits attributed to him exist as third person accounts, which for the most part he told on himself, but another spate of anecdotes dealt with him as a character, sometimes shiftless, sometimes boastful, sometimes sharp. "He never worked a day in his life that I can remember," recalled one critical acquaintance, "but he had done everything anyone else had—and twice as good, at least twice as good." In the same vein the skeptic added, "He musta been two hundred years old. Yeah, that's right,

'cause he worked twenty years in Arkansas, twenty years in Nebraska, twenty years in Iowa, thirty in Missouri, and I knew him
all my life."[136] Stamps did apparently spend some time in several of
these states. In one story he departs from his usual Munchausen
role to play the part of a slick watch trader.

SELLING A WATCH

Dan'l always wore a vest, and he carried a watch in every
pocket—the best watches in the country. I remember the last
trade he made, 'cause it was with John Patton. He sold John a
watch for a dollar, and it wasn't fifteen minutes 'fore John was
back with a dead watch. Dan'l looked at him and said, 'Damn it,
John, you just don't know how to carry a watch!'[137]

A complementary anecdote describes the one time Dan'l was
bested in a watch trade, by Victor Kremer, the teller, who discovered
Stamps's weakness for "wagon wheels," large old-fashioned silver
watches wound with a key, and traded Dan'l an ancient one for one
of Dan'l's best. "I got back at him all right, but it took me more than
ten years to do it," Vic acknowledged.

But the main theme of Dan'l's cycle dealt with hunting, fishing,
and farming wonders. He killed the biggest turtle ever seen in the
Illinois River, nine inches between the eyes, and after cleaning out
the meat paddled the shell across the river to Kampsville. He shot
a wagon-load of coons holed up in a sycamore stump. He owned a
half-banty hen that filled up a hole under a corn shock a foot deep
with eggs in one setting, until she rolled off the top of the pile. "Died
from overwork," he said when asked to show the banty. He also
owned a Jersey cow with such a big bag, Dan'l had to stand on a
scaffold to milk two teats on one side and two teats on the other. He
planted potatoes eight levels deep and then had to rent land on each
side of his farm to stack the yield.

One full text as recollected by a friend from Kampsville, catches
Dan'l in a tall-tale contest with a buddy.

BIG MOSQUITOES

Tony told 'bout how one day he was fishin' 'long the river. 'Fore
long he dozed off. He was layin' in the shade, but pretty soon the

sun moved and got in his eyes. As he woke up, he looked down
the river, and there was two big mosquitoes packin' a tree down
the bank. 'Bout that time a real big one flew over and scared the
two that was packin' the tree. So they dropped it. That tree fell a
hundred feet away from Tony, and it's a good thing it did. That
tree was so big it would have killed him if it fell any closer, the
branches spread out so far.

Well, Dan'l scratched his head and spit a couple of times, and
then he began. He wasn't goin' to be beat that easy! Seems as
though he was in Arkansas once and he was a'most broke. A
northern cattle buyer came into town and wanted Dan'l to find
him some steers. So next mornin' they started out through the
swamp. Pretty soon they heard a cow bell ringin', and they
started that way. When they got to a clearin', there was a mosquito standin' over his dead cow and ringin' its cow bell to beat
hell for the rest of the herd to come. Those mosquitoes were more
like coons than mosquitoes. You see, their toenails was so long
they could kick a cow in the belly and pierce its heart.[138]

Lies about the size and ferocity of mosquitoes outdo exaggerations
about any other animal, insect, or plant in American folklore.[139]
Dan'l's tall story about the mosquito killing the cow and ringing its
bell is reported in New Jersey and Arkansas. In a related whopper
mosquitoes eat a cow and pick their teeth with her horns. The best
known mosquito lie tells of the man who hides under a kettle to
escape the insects, they drill through it with their bills, he clinches
their bills, and they fly off with the kettle.[140] Though not included
in the sampling of Daniel Stamps's yarns, it is told by Jones Tracy.
Relating a widespread folktale unconnected with the hero's powers
does not notably assist his legend, but in this case Dan'l uses the lie
to best another liar, and so enhance his reputation as a fabulist. We
have seen Jones Tracy likewise top a rival.

As with other Munchausens, Dan'l divided his repertoire between
brags about his success as hunter, fisherman, and farmer, and stock
fictions in which he was merely the observer. In the manner of
Oregon Smith, he related marvels he had beheld while residing in
other states.

BURYING CORPSES IN POST HOLES

One winter out in Iowa the cholera broke out, and the ther-
mometer stayed down at twenty below for two months. It was

really bad, 'cause sometimes a whole family would be wiped out. Anyhow, everyone was afraid of the dead ones, so they stacked them in a loft, waitin' till the ground thawed so they could bury them. Dan'l said when Spring came they just dug post holes and buried them stiffs standing up. If the tall ones were too long for the holes, they just sharpened their toes a little and drove them the rest of the way down.

That same winter a guy died where Dan'l himself was stayin'. He died upstairs, and everyone was afraid to go near him. Dan'l decided to dig a hole right outside the window and drop the guy in it. When he pushed this guy out the window, he landed on his feet, and it must of jarred the life back in him, 'cause he just walked away.[141]

In Idaho and Alberta the living reportedly drove frozen corpses into the hard ground with sledges, so Dan'l is again tapping traditional windies.[142] By drawing on his out-of-state travels he could incorporate into his repertoire tales about the extreme cold of Iowa and the extreme heat of Arkansas, where corn started to pop while he was cutting it and fell to the ground like snow, causing his horses to shiver and shake.

Enough of the tall tales and anecdotes linked to Daniel Stamps have been recorded by Walker from the river country of western Illinois to document the persistence of yet another Munchausen folk hero in the American grain, remembered for the remarkable yarns he told about what he had done and seen.

EIGHT

Hathaway Jones
(1870–1937)

A regional writer in 1941, portraying Oregon and Washington, lingered over a character named Hathaway Jones, "whose imaginary exploits illustrating his own courage, strength, and ingenuity have made him one of the immortal yarners of the Pacific Northwest."[143] Hathaway had died four years earlier at fifty-eight, falling over a cliff from his mule while pursuing his hazardous occupation as the last mail carrier in the United States to operate with a mule team, but his tales, and tales told about him, lived on in the Rogue River mountain wilderness of southwestern Oregon. Proud of his reputation as the biggest liar in the country, he reportedly threatened to sue the Portland *Oregonian* for assigning the honor to someone else.

A few squibs about Hathaway drifted into print following this 1941 sketch, chiefly in local publications, although the *Saturday Evening Post* gave him mention in a 1946 issue.[144] Reminiscing in 1954 about mining experiences in the Rogue Canyon half a century before, Claude Riddle set down his impressions of Hathaway, who was bringing him pack supplies, and included a dozen of Jones's yarns in his book *In the Happy Hills,* published in Roseburg, Oregon, where Hathaway's grandfather Isaac had once operated a flour mill. Riddle thus recalls the mail carrier:

> He was small and short and walked with a forward stoop. His
> arms were long and his hands seemed to swing ahead below his
> knees. . . . He wore a conical little black hat with a buckskin
> string woven in for a headband. His heavy blue flannel shirt was
> open and black hair decorated his throat and breast. . . . Hatha-
> way's speech was most peculiar—a cross between a harelip and
> tonguetie.[145]

In 1974 an historian from Oregon, Stephen Dow Beckham, capti-
vated by the Rogue River country, assembled Hathaway Jones's repertoire under the title, *Tall Tales from Rogue River, The Yarns of
Hathaway Jones*. Not having access to the living Munchausen,
Beckham relied on two manuscript collections and the few local
publications, and recorded several retellers of Hathaway's tales who
hunted and fished along Rogue River and had heard Hathaway stories. His major source proved to be the unpublished collection of a
retired attorney from San Francisco, Arthur Dorn, who had moved
to Agness on the Rogue River close to the sea during the Depression
to fish, hunt, garden and translate Buddhist sutras. As a side
amusement Dorn wrote down many of the stories he heard Hathaway relate when delivering mail at Agness between 1936 and 1941,
intending to contribute them to an Oregon Folklore Project contem-
plated but never published by the WPA. Dorn altered the yarns from
first to third person and suppressed Jones's dialect, hence his versions of the narratives fail to represent the mail carrier's style, but
they do convey the substance and extent of his repertoire and supply
valuable ethnographic background. Dorn collected not only from
Hathaway but from half a dozen Rogue River residents and part-
time guides who relished repeating Jone's gems. Beckham names
and identifies this network of southwestern Oregon folk who maintained the tall-tale and comic anecdote cycle during Hathaway's
lifetime and after his death. For instance, a long-time lodge proprietor at Agness, Larry Lucas, skillfully mimicked Jones's harelip
stutter and nasal twang.

These multiple sources yield several versions for various of the 44
texts Hathaway Jones told about himself. Eleven stories come with
two variants, two stories with three variants, another two with four
variants, while "The Rolling Stone" tops them all with five, a total
of forty-one variants for sixteen tales, good evidence of their circulation. Beckham also presents single versions of eleven tales Hath-

away told about his grandfather Ike and three about his father Sampson, from whom he inherited his remarkable propensities.

Some themes in Hathaway's narratives, such as the Great Hunter, the Great Fisherman, and the Great Farmer, echo brags of his fellow Munchausens. More specific to Hathaway's doings are the Great Mail Carrier and the Great Miner. In two of his most renowned achievements he acts as Builder of the Great Fireplace. Another way of dividing up Hathaway's tales could be along the lines of the dramatis personae: wild animals, such as bears and wild hogs; domestic animals, primarily mules, plus an assortment of curious pets; and supercilious outsiders venturing into the Rogue River country, whom Hathaway always managed to discomfit.

This country in which Hathaway lived and about which he yarned bore some resemblance to Bridger's Rocky Mountain West in its wild and rugged character. In 1930 scarcely three thousand persons lived in Curry County, mostly along the fifty miles of southern Oregon coastline, and few penetrated into its forest-covered mountains and winding river canyons. Transportation on the Rogue River depended on boats that "scoop their way through the gravel up the roaring, rocky, and, in many places, uncomfortably shallow river."[146]

To what extent Hathaway injected accounts of the rough conditions in the lower Rogue River country into his tales we cannot be sure, since so many of the texts as we now have them contain extensive descriptive settings supplied by Arthur Dorn, who converts Hathaway's concise personal experiences into elaborate third person adventures. One text attributed directly to Hathaway by a re-teller is the shortest in the collection and suggests Jones's style:

> Hathaway said: "One day I came along here and there were seven deer in that little draw. One of them was as black as coal. I had never seen a black deer, so I shot that one, and when I come up to him I see he was just a mass of fleas."[147]

The other version, from the Dorn Collection, runs to 270 as opposed to 52 words, does not place the tale in Hathaway's mouth, and supplies information about the deadly nature of ticks which in the Rogue River country fastened on some deer and ignored others. What oral tradition loses, ethnography gains. Dorn's additions convey a sense of the mountain and canyon wilderness, the varmints that roamed the area, and the hardy souls, with a strong Indian admixture, who contended with the varmints and the rigors of nature. Recurrent place names in the yarns—Agness, Illahe, Gold Beach, Curry County—help create a little world in the back of beyond. According to Nancy Wilson Ross, Gold Beach on the Pacific shore, the outlet of the Rogue River, represents "one of the last stands of frontier independence, self-sufficiency, and homely eccentricity to be found in America."[148] Yet to Hathaway it offered his one opportunity for excitement on the rare occasions he left his inland haunts.

Background milieu provided by Arthur Dorn gives us a picture of Hathaway Jones's manner of living. He would spend stormy winter months up river in an abandoned miner's cabin, trapping and idling, and planting potatoes on a hillside. In the summer he traipsed down to Gold Beach to go salmon fishing. Late in the fall he returned to the cabin carrying on his back three packhorse loads of supplies and, to occupy his hands, a fifty pound sack of flour under each arm. He would never use a pack mule to bring in winter provisions, although he had six in his pasture, plus a riding mule. Thus laden, he walked forty miles upriver in a day, ignoring the pouring rains.[149] According to Hathaway, "You don't never ketch cold if'n yer dry yer clothes without taken 'em off."[150]

The Great Hunter and Fisherman

Forest creatures abound in Hathaway's yarns, and he constantly and casually hunts, shoots and kills bear, deer, wild hogs, cougars, raccoons, rattlesnakes, geese, and skunks. A number of his hunting exploits deal with slow bullets that take considerable time to reach their destination, but never miss their target. He once fired his old buffalo gun at noon toward a flock of honker geese out of sight in the sky, and when the sun was setting a fat goose with its head cut off crashed through the roof. Another time Hathaway fired at a big buck half a mile away on a mountain, then remembered he had used slow black powder instead of the new smokeless powder. He reloaded with the new shells and dropped the deer. Hastening up the mountain to dress the buck, he reached the animal, bent over with his knife to bleed her, and felt a sting in his rear. The slow bullet had just caught up with him. But again it might be the quickness of the

Hathaway Jones and the Flying Bear

prey rather than the slowness of the bullet that evoked wonder, as in this yarn by one who knew Hathaway.

THE FAST DEER

Another of the group asked Hathaway about a deer that had been shot seven times. "Were you mad at that there forked horn, harelip, 'er was you feelin' you had too many cartridges?"

"Only shot 'em one time," snarled Hathaway. "Jumped 'im up in the open timber 'tother side of Skunk Cabbage Flat, and he lit out dodgin' trees like a bat out-a hell. Jest as he dodged a great big fir tree I shot 'im right through the heart, but he ran quite a ways 'fore he drapped. Well sir, he run so fast, dodging trees this away and that away, my bullet jest went in and out a-makin' all them holes."[151]

Like Davy Crockett of the Tennessee canebrakes and Jim Doggett in *The Big Bear of Arkansas,* Hathaway Jones was "numerous in b'ar hunts." Varied were the expedients to which he resorted when meeting bruin in the forest. When a bear he had wounded chased Hathaway out on a long limb extending over a five hundred foot cliff, Hathaway yelled at him, "Go back, you damn fool! This limb will break and we will both get killed!" In a similar situation, Hathaway leaped from the limb to safety, the slim fir tree snapped back and threw the bear across the canyon into another slim tree, which bent and tossed him back into the first. So the bear was tossed back and forth, until Hathaway cut down the first tree while the bear was in midflight. The bear changed its course and landed in a larger, stronger tree, which bent and threw the bear across the canyon into a comparable tree. This routine kept up with Hathaway cutting bear-bouncing trees and the bear shifting to bigger ones, until a very large tree threw the bear over the top of the mountain, four thousand feet high. A stranger in the Agness post office doubted Hathaway's yarn. Hathaway curled one side of his harelip and responded tolerantly, "Wouldn't expect a tenderfoot to believe me, but I can take you to the young fir tree I chopped down. What better proof would a man with any sense want?"[152]

If Hathaway always bested bears, in one bear hunt a mule bested him.

The Bear, the Deer, and the Mule

"My wife Florey said to me," Hathaway would begin, " 'You better go out and shoot us a deer. We haven't got a bit of meat in the cabin for breakfast!'

"I hadn't gone but a little piece before I shot a five-hundred-pound bear. That bear was the fattest thing you ever saw. The grease run right out the bullet hole and down the hill for fifty feet. Well, I threw him on my mule and started home. Part way along I come across a deer. So I shot him, too, threw him up on top the bear and packed on down to the river.

"And then that durned old mule balked. Seeing how I couldn't get him to cross, I threw the deer and the bear on my back and started swimming. Halfway over, I noticed I was swimming

deeper than usual, and I looked around. You know, that darned
mule was setting up on top the bear."[153]

Hathaway talked more about hunting than fishing, but the Year
of the Big Freeze did see him perform an extraordinary exploit as
fisherman. The ice on Rogue River turned so thick cattle and horses
crossed upon it, and Hathaway walked on it, but fell through. His
heavy clothing carried him to the bottom, and as he walked along
the river bed he spotted a big Chinook salmon and grabbed its tail.
The fish pulled him so fast the friction warmed his body. Seeing a
hole in the ice the salmon jumped through it, Hathaway hanging on
behind. Once on top the ice Hathaway threw the fish over his shoulders and carried it home for supper, bracing himself on the trail
with a big stick he picked up. Arriving at his cabin, he set the stick
against the wall, but on thawing, the stick proved to be a snake.[154]

The Great Farmer

Hathaway related extended narratives about his experiments
planting potatoes and melons. The smallest potato in his potato
patch weighed ten pounds, and the crop proved so big and long he
corded them in ricks like stovewood over an acre and a half of
land.[155] His melons averaged three hundred pounds apiece, and he
harvested fifty tons from one acre. Because the vines dragged the
melons after them and wore them down, Hathaway tied sleds to the
vines, put wheels on the sleds, and then stood by his fence and
watched the melons move and grow.[156]

The Great Mail Carrier

In the course of carrying letters, tools, Monkey Ward's catalogues,
political circulars and mail order clothing to the scattered homes in
the Rogue wilderness, Hathaway had to battle rugged terrain and
fierce weather, which lent themselves to fabulous narratives—not
entirely fabulous, since Hathaway met his death on the mail route
plunging over a cliff. Writing of the winters Hathaway carried mail
over the Rogue River Trail and across Nine Mile Mountain to West
Fort, Dorn refers to torrential downpours that caused landslides
covering the trail for miles with mud and slush into which the pack

mules sank almost to their bellies; to snowflakes large as a man's hand; to blizzards and windstorms forming great snowdrifts. From such realities evolved Hathaway's yarns of deep snows and great freezes. He built one tale around a giant snowdrift blocking his path which even the mules could not negotiate. Hathaway saw a large pine tree in an open space between drifts, and led his fastest mule to the tree. With encouraging words he urged her to run around it faster and faster, until she became a red-hot blur. Then he drove her through the drift so she would melt a passageway for the pack train to follow.[157]

In the Winter of the Big Snow, Hathaway abandoned his mule and walked thirty miles into the snow, which piled ever higher until it reached above his head, and a passerby would only see a hat bobbing on top the drift. Up above he could hear the voices of families waiting for him to deliver the mail, and (according to Hathaway, no doubt saying this with a straight face) they abused him for being late, and even imitated his harelip way of talking (all this behind his back, and over his head). Finally he came out of the snow at Ilahe and frightened an old squaw gathering fir bark. "Old fat squaw run faster'n a horse!" Hathaway commented to end his saga.[158]

In another narrative of a big snow, rendered by Dorn with majestic details, a fierce snowstorm caused one of the mules to lose its footing and slip down the mountainside, scattering the whole pack to which it was hitched and strewing the goods all over the slope. Four years later riding along the same trail in summer, Hathaway noticed a white object in a pine tree fifty-one feet high. He climbed the tree and retrieved a side of bacon "just as sweet and fresh as it was the day it left the store." The snow had crested to the treetop.

The Great Miner

Two yarns reflect the gold fever that once swept the Rogue country. As a youth Hathaway heard prospectors at Agness talking about gold they had discovered at Mule Creek, and he went prospecting himself. He found gold so rich it was hanging in melted columns, so soft you could bend it like soap. But his father dissuaded him from mining the lode, saying, "Well, son, that's too far from the railroad."

Three variants relate how Hathaway struck a lode of gold so rich he could not drill the rock. Here he is telling a group of the boys drinking moonshine, from whom he had borrowed a single jack and drill, that he had uncovered the biggest gold mine in the world.

HATHAWAY'S RICH LODE

"Did't I tell you 'boutin' them holes in that there ledge? I drilled 'em 'fore I brung back yer tools, but when I got home fer powder to blast 'em there weren't none. Paw done used it all up blastin' salmon down in the mouth of the crick. Sure raised hell with the salmon. Got 'nough to salt down a bar' full. 'Twas a long time 'fore Paw got some powder brung up from Gold Beach.

"Well, drilled them holes last May, an' went up to blast 'em out here about a week back, but when I come to 'em they weren't no room fer the powder. They was filled up with gold so the powder wouldn't go in. Gold was oozin' outen them holes and dreein' down the mountain plum t' the crick. Weren't nothin' I could do so I jest says to myself—to hell with 'em."[159]

All three variants speak of the gold oozing out of the drill holes, a motif also reported from California.

The Great Wag

The people who appear in the yarns, with somewhat less frequency than the animals and birds, fall into two groups: Hathaway's wilderness–smart Rogue River cronies, and various arrogant outsiders, in the traditional contrast presented on earlier frontiers between the backwoodsman and the effete alien. Just as Jim Bridger fended off inquisitive onlookers with extravagant untruths, so did Hathaway Jones play the game of "fool the dude." When six city men from Portland hired him as a deer-hunting guide—again like Bridger, Jones enjoyed a reputation as "the most famous hunting guide on the Rogue"[160]—they thought to best him in a lying contest and tried some fishing whoppers on great runs of steelhead they had seen. Hathaway calmly responded that in these parts steelhead were so thick in the water that there was no room for the water. When an inquisitive Easterner he was guiding on a big game hunt inquired about what had caused the holes in the trail by the Devil's Stairway, Hathaway stated he had sunk into the solid rock there under the weight of seven big bucks he was carrying. Queried closely in Gold Beach as to why he was broke, by a city dude paying for his drinks, Jones declared that he never worked, although he was "the strongest and healthiest man on the lower Rogue." "Then why can't you work?" insisted the stranger. Hathaway told him exercise developed his muscles so fast they split his skin. One time two "bright young city investigators" representing the Oregon Game Commission made their way nervously to Hathaway's cabin to arrest him for shooting old doe the year round, although everybody on the Rogue fed his dogs on doe and hogs. Hathaway welcomed them and set a pot of doe stew on the table, but when he picked up his rifle they fled in haste. Another time "a wealthy dog fancier," who was also "a big game hunter from Virginia," hired Hathaway as a guide. After losing his pack of prize Airedales to a wily bear, the sportsman bought Hathaway's hounds Towser and Nellie and took them to Virginia. Pining for their master, the hounds made their way back to Hathaway's cabin, on a two-year journey, raising a family of green-and yellow-eyed pups en route. In all these encounters with the outside world, Hathaway scores triumphs over the intruders from the urban culture.

The Great Builder

Two of Hathaway's most repeated yarns, "The Magnificent Fireplace" and "The Rolling Stone," credit his powers for building a log cabin, with special emphasis upon the chimney, the fireplace, and the mantel above the fireplace. Some versions provide elaborate details on the building of the cabin and the fireplace, but all emphasize the great drawing power of the fireplace. In one text Hathaway builds the fireplace; in two his father is the builder; and once the two build it together. Here Hathaway gives the credit to his dad.

THE MAGNIFICENT FIREPLACE

"Pa, he built this fireplace and boy did that fireplace draw. You never seen a fireplace like that. He shut the door and built a fire in this fireplace and the first thing it did, it drew the door right off the hinges, sent it up the chimney. The old hound dog bitch was about to have puppies was tied to the post of the porch and then she came right behind that door; it pulled four pups right out of her and before we could put out the fire, we had two more! That's drawing."[161]

In other renditions Hathaway and his dad pile firewood in the back yard, light the fire, open the back door, and let the fireplace draw in wood. Fireplaces with comparable drawing power are reported from Vermont, New Hampshire, and New York.[162]

Complementing "The Magnificent Fireplace" is the tale of "The Rolling Stone," the only yarn reported in five versions. Hathaway needed a round rock to complete the mantel over the fireplace, and he obtained it by pushing a precariously balanced ten-ton boulder down a steep canyon. The boulder splashed into the creek and bounded up the other side of the mountain, tossing brush and trees around like feathers, and kept repeating its journey up and down, growing smaller all the time. Finally when it was worn down to the size of the hole on the mantel, round as a buckshot, Hathaway made his move:

> "Had me a leetle trouble ketchin' 'er, scooped 'er up in a sack, when she war passin'. Damned if'n she didn't keep right on spinnin' and hummin' all the way home, but soon's I got 'er in that hole, she kinder slowed down."[163]

The heroic Jones that emerges from his yarns shares features with other American Munchausens and yet retains a distinctive quality. Some of his whoppers belong to them as well: Oregon Smith and Jones Tracy also sink into solid rock; Gib Morgan also sells wooden shoe pegs for oats and recovers his watch months after dropping it down an oil well to find it keeping perfect time (Hathaway dropped his in a sixty foot snowbank). But much of his repertoire and style are his own. The twang and stutter resulting from his harelip made even more memorable his imagery: "meaner than cat dung;" "the still sow gets the swill;" "making more noise than driving a four-horse team through the woods dragging a bull-hide." While other of his fellow braggarts also hunted, fished, farmed, cut timber, and guided sportsmen, only Hathaway carried the mails over nearly impassable trails. Hathaway Jones drew his long bows on America's last frontier.

Afterword

Jeff Dorson

DURING the last six months of my father's life, I was able to work closely with him on a number of projects. After my college graduation I began to take interest in my father's writing and work and to help him with his correspondence and eventually his research. Above all, he needed help in completing the five books he proposed to finish in the year ahead. During the summer of 1981 he sent three of his intended five books off to publishers. Indiana University Press received this manuscript; *The Land of the Millrats: Folklore of the Calumet Region* was written for Harvard University Press; and the last work edited by him, *The Handbook of American Folklore,* is also being issued by Indiana University Press.

We worked well together and became fast friends. One summer night we talked at length about the possibility of our teaming up to do collecting and research. He reminded me that Alan Lomax traveled through Texas with his father, collecting folktales from black prisoners and folksongs from cowboys, and together they produced *Negro Folk Songs as Sung by Lead Belly* (New York, 1936). The very next morning after our talk he collapsed on the tennis court and lapsed into a coma that lasted two and a half months and from which he never awoke. My mother and I were with him when he finally passed away Friday afternoon, September 11, 1981.

Though I lack formal training as a folklorist, I was nurtured on

170

the principles of the discipline from an early age. I remember few of the nursery rhymes told to me, but I do recall hearing that Paul Bunyan did not belong in the body of American folklore because he had no rich oral tradition of his own. He and his blue ox, Babe, were created solely out of commercial interest and exist as an example of a contrived, romantic cousin of folklore that my father labeled "fakelore." To the ghosts, demons, and sea-serpents I feared as a child were added the evils of fakelore.

Dad was a talented storyteller and demonstrated the skills of the rustic yarn-spinner. He could draw from his repertoire full of anecdotes, windies, jokes, tall tales, and superstitions. His favorite bedtime stories were of his own creation. He invented the character Hucus Blucus, an incorrigible young trouble-maker fashioned after the likes of Huckleberry Finn and Peck's Bad Boy. In keeping with many storytelling traditions, Dad would gesture wildly with his hands to impart emphasis or paint the scene, create new characters from his facial expressions, and make up silly words to give his story a mock literary flavor. His stories were always extravagant because he meshed various traditions, borrowing freely from wonder tales, folk drama, Old World beliefs, and Yankee boasts. The stories he told were never long-winded, and sometimes he quieted our pleas for more by simply giving us motif-numbers.

Like any good father, he was also keen to pass on to his children some of the lessons he learned in life. I learned early to appreciate the value of good humor. I especially enjoyed hearing the cycle of the Yankee trickster tales performed by our early American folk heroes. I remember Dad telling me how Davy Crockett fooled the bartender by paying for his new drinks with the same coonskin. "A shot of whiskey, Sam!" Davy would say, grinning broadly to the bartender, slamming his fist hard against the counter. To pay for his drinks Davy would present a fine-looking coonskin to the bartender. But as soon as the bartender would turn to another customer, Davy would reach over the counter, take back his coonskin, and begin the bartering process all over.

Second, I learned how important it was to Dad always to be prepared. "Whenever you are to give a paper or speech," he told me when I was still in grade school, "always bring a book, preferably one you have written." "And never," he told me when I was entering junior high school, "forget your class notes before you begin to lecture." Only now do I realize that in most of our early conversations he was talking to himself.

Neither the tape recorder nor the movie projector ever worked during his classroom presentations. But to compensate he found that holding up one of his books usually worked as well. "So which one of your books do you refer to when the projector doesn't work?" I asked one day. "Any one of them. They are all so good!" he replied.

Of course, I was also exposed to his serious side. His interest in the study of comic heroes and beasts grew from a paper he delivered at a conference entitled "Creatures of Legendry," in Omaha, Nebraska, in the fall of 1978. He had carried this curiosity with him from his undergraduate and graduate days at Harvard. He had discovered frontier humor and the oral tall-tale tradition by reading Mark Twain and Constance Rourke's *American Humor* (1931). Dad's first publication was a collection of Davy Crockett almanacs from the 1830s, 40s, and 50s entitled *Davy Crockett, American Comic Legend* (1946). Davy Crockett became special property of the American almanacs, which transformed him from a great patriarch and frontiersman into the "gamecock of the wilderness," a coarse, outrageous ring-tailed roarer, the precursor and prototype of the eight Munchausens described in this book.

Man and Beast in American Comic Legend began to take shape with two chapters published in *American Folklore*. The hoopsnake and other exotic creatures living in marvel tales on the tongues of European travelers are mentioned in the chapter entitled "Colonial Folklore." But the descriptions of these fearsome creatures changed after the Colonial period. Historical developments altered the character of U. S. folklore, a minor theme in this book and the prevailing thesis in *America in Legend*. After the wilderness was tamed, the New World's gruesome fabled animals took on comic qualities, as the illustrations in this text show. In another chapter from *American Folklore,* entitled "A Gallery of Folk Heroes," Dad surveyed the ranks of the autobiographical sagamen. In this edition he filled out his original list to include Len Henry, Jones Tracy, Daniel Stamps, and Hathaway Jones. Although all of them fancied themselves conquering heroes, their feats are all too often deflated by exaggeration, dialect, malapropisms, and ridiculous word coinage.

A new American identity was expressed in comic legends. European tales of "The Marvelous Hunt" transplanted themselves in our body of comic folklore, but most comic traditions of Europeans, Native Americans, and Afro-Americans did not strongly influence our native folk humor, which grew alongside our national pride. Boasting of the ugly, outrageous, and preposterous was a favorite device of our early homespun humorists. The backroad liars flaunted the confidence of a new nation and fed upon the disdain of the European aristocrats and New England dandies. Almost overnight folk demi-gods pushed their way into our national mythology. Charging after them into the pantheon came our comic beasts, many of whom sprung out of tall tales, commercialism, and the Yankee imagination.

We look to the folklorist to record and preserve variants of oral traditions, but he or she is also needed to remind us of the part of our literary inheritance that is forgotten. One of America's oldest forms of satire and ridicule, our native folk humor, left us this legacy of marvel tales of comic beasts and bumpkin heroes, which Dad identified as he combed through dime jest books, travelogues, local publications, and Western yarns.

The study of American intellectual history often omits the study of folk history; then the appreciation of ballads, anecdotes, and comic legends is lost, and an important part of our heritage is overlooked. To combine the study of common culture and high culture was one of Dad's passions and a recurrent theme in a number of his books. It was presented most forcefully and eloquently in his article "The Value of the Humanities," from *The Humanist as Citizen* (Chapel Hill: University of North Carolina Press, 1981). He charged the humanities with elitism for disavowing folklore as a separate but related area of study and for excluding from its research the achievements of the common folk. The materials of folklore, he reminded us, can bridge the history of the non-elite and that of the elite: "As folk history counter-balances intellectual history, so will oral literature counterbalance art literature, folk religion counter the great creeds, folk art counter the fine arts, folk speech counter the king's English" (p. 166).

My own interest in folklore led me to read as many of Dad's books as I could in the short time that I worked with him. His literary style did not change much in the thirty years he spent writing on folklore, nor did the energy he poured into the cause slacken. Discovering a new vein of oral tales—whether it was in the Upper

Peninsula, where he did his first research, or in the steel mills of Gary, Indiana—was always an important event, and his finds would usually become a new book. The Upper Peninsula trip produced *Bloodstoppers and Bearwalkers* (1952). His Gary venture yielded *Land of the Millrats*.

His standards were high. He always collected and wrote with precision, making sure that his would be a generation of trained researchers and that folklore's fragile reputation would never again be damaged by writers with unreliable methodologies. Many American authors who mistakenly called themselves folklorists rewrote what they heard and proffered folktales in the form of children's stories or bound them up in a treasury and handed them out in that kind of sweetened version. Thus was folklore weakened by literary adaptation. Folktales that appeared in print lost their spirit; their coarseness, spontaneity, and freshness were missing.

Dad was the doyen of his field. For thirty years he gave shape to the course of American folklore and was sought out by historians and folklorists from every continent. I am confident that his works will endure and that he left the discipline in capable hands. His colleagues and former students will continue to advance the study of folklore in my father's tradition of honesty and artistry.

Jeff Dorson

October 1981

NOTES

Part I. American Legendary Creatures

1. Richard M. Dorson, *Folklore and Fakelore* (Cambridge: Harvard University Press, 1976), p. 186; Sean O'Sullivan, *Folktales of Ireland* (Chicago and London: University of Chicago Press, 1966), the tale of Sean Palmer, pp. 209–220.

2. Richard M. Dorson, *Folk Legends of Japan* (Rutland, Vermont, and Tokyo: Charles E. Tuttle, 1962), pp. 63–65.

3. Edward W. Lane, *An Account of the Manners and Customs of the Modern Egyptians* [1836] (New York: Dover, 1973), pp. 427–428.

4. Martha Blache, "Structural Analysis of Guarani Memorates and Anecdotes" (Indiana University dissertation, November 1977).

5. Walker D. Wyman, *Mythical Creatures of the North Country* (River Falls, Wis.: River Falls State University Press, 1969), pp. v–vi.

6. William T. Cox, *Fearsome Creatures of the Lumberwoods* (Washington, D.C.: Judd and Detweiler, 1910), Introduction. Cox's book is reprinted in Wyman, pp. 27–65, and in part in B. A. Botkin, *A Treasury of American Folklore* (New York: Crown, 1944), pp. 377–78, 648–50 [six creatures].

7. Cox, p. 21.

8. Henry H. Tryon, *Fearsome Critters* (Cornwall, N.Y.: Idlewild Press, 1939), p. 18.

9. Cox, p. 33.

10. Curtis MacDougall, *Hoaxes* (New York: Macmillan, 1940), p. 15; Cox, p. 45.

11. MacDougall, p. 15; Cox, p. 11.

12. MacDougall, facing page 24.

13. Alvin Schwartz, *Kickle Snifters and Other Fearsome Critters, Collected from American Folklore* (Philadelphia and New York: J. B. Lippincott, 1976), 64 pages.

14. Ibid., p. 62.

15. Cox, p. 15.

16. Charles E. Brown, *Paul Bunyan Natural History* (Madison: Wisconsin Folklore Society, 1935).

17. Charles M. Skinner, *American Myths and Legends* (Philadelphia and London: J. B. Lippincott, 1903), Vol. I, p. 35.

18. Ibid., p. 37.

19. Lillian Marsh Higbee, *Bacchus of Windham and The Frog Fright* (n.p., 1930), p. 14 [26-page booklet].

20. *The Rev. Samuel Peters' LL.D. General History of Connecticut,* ed. Samuel J. McCormick (New York: Irvington, 1977), pp. 129–131.

21. Higbee, p. 15.

22. Higbee, p. 19, quoting Ellen D. Larned, *History of Windham County, Conn.* (Worcester, Mass., 1874), I, 261.

23. Ibid.

24. Higbee, pp. 21, 23.

25. Larned, I, 562–563.

26. Thomas R. Hazard, *The Jonny-Cake Papers of "Shepard Tom"* (Boston, 1915), pp. 361–362.

27. Charles M. Skinner, *Myths and Legends of Our Own Land* (Philadelphia, 1896), I, 40–41. Skinner follows Peters in the erroneous date of 1758.

28. *Windham's Bi-Centennial 1692–1892* (Hartford, Conn., 1893), pp. 95–107.

29. Higbee, p. 17.

30. Larned, I, 562.

31. Ernest W. Baughman, *Type and Motif-Index of the Folktales of England and North America* (The Hague: Mouton, 1966), pp. 316–317. Several examples are given in Richard M. Dorson, *Jonathan Draws the Long Bow* (Cambridge: Harvard University Press, 1946), p. 19.

32. William Bartram, *Travels through North and South Carolina. . . .* (Philadelphia, 1791), p. 90, cited in James R. Masterson, "Travelers' Tales of Colonial Natural History," *Journal of American Folklore* 59 (1946):59.

33. All references in this paragraph, save for Bartram, are from Robert T. Clark, "The Literary Growth of the Louisiana Bullfrog," in *Mexican Border Ballads and Other Lore,* ed. Mody C. Boatright, Publications of the Texas Folk-Lore Society 21 (Austin, 1946), pp. 105–111.

34. Roy Bedicheck, "Folklore in Natural History," *Texas Folk and Folklore,* ed. Mody C. Boatright, Publications of the Texas Folklore Society 26 (Dallas: Southern Methodist University Press, 1954), pp. 301–303. The last swallowing is cited from Osmond P. Bereland, *Animal Facts and Fancies* (New York, 1948), p. 182.

35. Bernard DeVoto, *Mark Twain's America* (Boston: Little, Brown, 1932), pp. 340–342; cf. pp. 172–178 for a discussion of this "folk tale of the Mississippi frontier."

36. Bernard DeVoto, *Mark Twain at Work* (Cambridge: Harvard University Press, 1942), p. 68, quoted in B. J. Whiting, "Gyuscutus, Royal Nonesuch and Other Hoaxes," *Southern Folklore Quarterly* 8 (1944):246 n.38.

37. Whiting, p. 273.

38. Ibid., citing DeLancey Ferguson, *Mark Twain: Man and Legend* (Indianapolis: Bobbs-Merrill, 1943), p. 81.

39. Francis A. Durivage and George P. Burnham, *Stray Subjects Arrested and Bound Over* (Philadelphia: Carey and Hart, 1848), p. 62.

40. *The Spirit of the Times* 15 (1845):370, reprinted in Whiting, p. 265.

41. Federal Writers Project, *Chillicothe and Ross County* (n.p.: The Ross County Northwest Territory Committee, 1938), pp. 29–30.

42. Vance Randolph, *We Always Lie to Strangers* (New York: Columbia University Press, 1951), pp. 41–46. Drawing on page 42.

43. Brown, pp. 86–87.

44. Randolph, pp. 64–65.

45. Schwartz, p. 62, gives all these names except for sidehill winder (Skinner), wampus cat (Brown, Wyman), and rackabore (MacDougall).

46. Reprinted in Richard M. Dorson, "Yorker Yarns of Yore," *New York Folklore Quarterly* 3 (1947):23–27.

47. Lake Shore Kearney, *The Hodag, And other Tales of the Logging Camps* (Wausau, Wis., 1928), pp. 34–35.

48. Fred L. Holmes, *Badger Saints and Sinners* (Milwaukee: E. M. Hale,

1939), p. 473, quoting Martin Fitzgerald, a contemporary lumber cruiser for Brown Brothers of Rhinelander, Wisconsin.

49. Randolph, pp. 61–62.

50. Skinner, *American Myths and Legends,* vol. I, pp. 35–36.

51. Brown, p. 5.

52. *Follow de Drinkin Gou'd,* ed. J. Frank Dobie, Publications of the Texas Folk-Lore Society 7 (Austin, 1928), pp. 38–40.

53. Roger Welsch, *Shingling the Fog And Other Plains Lies* (Chicago: Sage Books, The Swallow Press, 1972), pp. 88–89.

54. Ibid.

55. Eugene Hammel, "The Side Hill Guanos," *Western Folklore* 10 (1951):322.

56. Harold W. Thompson, *Body, Boots and Britches* (Philadelphia: Lippincott, 1940), p. 273.

57. Tryon, pp. 39–40.

58. Ibid., pp. 40–41.

59. Esther Shephard, *Paul Bunyan* (New York: Harcourt, Brace, 1924), pp. 28–30.

60. Baughman, p. 533: Motifs x138.1* and x1382*.

61. Richard M. Dorson, *Jonathan Draws the Long Bow* (Cambridge: Harvard University Press, 1946), pp. 95–96, from the *Exeter* (N.H.) *News Letter,* June 15, 1841; also the New York *Spirit of the Times* 13 (Dec. 23, 1843):506.

62. Randolph, pp. 21–22.

63. Cox, p. 9.

64. Horace P. Beck, "The Animal that Cannot Lie Down," *Journal of the Washington Academy of Sciences* 39:9 (1949):294–301.

65. Given in Beck, p. 295.

66. James Kenney, "Journal Begun . . . 1761," ed., John W. Jordan, *Pennsylvania Magazine of History and Biography* 37 (1913):42, quoted in James R. Masterson, "Travelers' Tales of Colonial Natural History," *Journal of American Folklore* 59 (1946):55.

67. Tryon, p. 29.

68. Schwartz, pp. 22–23.

69. Cox, p. 29.

70. Kearney, p. 12.

71. Kearney, p. 93.

72. Brown, p. 4.

73. Holmes, p. 460.

74. Ibid., pp. 465–466.

75. Tryon, p. 25, cf. the Squonk, p. 49; Cox, p. 31.

76. MacDougall, pp. 17–18. The photograph of the hodag faces page 25.

77. Robert Gard and L. C. Sorden, *Wisconsin Lore, Antics and Anecdotes of Wisconsin People and Places* (New York: Duell, Sloan and Pearce, 1962), pp. 245–260.

78. Wyman, p. 4.

79. Data taken from John Gutowski, "The Protofestival: Local Guide to American Folk Behavior," *Journal of the Folklore Institute* 15 (1978):113–131. The quotations are from pages 116, 121, 123, 140–142. The Philosopher's catch-tale is given in Gutowski, "American Folklore and the Modern American Community Festival: A Case Study of Turtle Days in Churubusco, Indiana" (Indiana University doctoral dissertation in folklore,

Bloomington, 1977), pp. 140–142. This dissertation contains a number of photographs of the Turtle Days Festival.

80. Wyman, pp. 4–5.

81. Reprinted in Richard M. Dorson, ed., *America Begins* (New York: Pantheon, 1950), pp. 93–94.

82. Masterson, p. 181.

83. John F. D. Smith, *A Tour in the United States of America* (London, 1784), I, 264–265, quoted in Masterson, p. 181.

84. Quoted in Masterson, p. 182.

85. "Skitt" (Harden E. Taliaferro), *Fisher's River (North Carolina) Scenes and Characters* (New York: Harper and Brothers, 1859), pp. 55–58. Illustrated by John M'Lenan.

86. *Idaho Lore,* prepared by the Federal Writers' Project of the Work Projects Administration, Vardis Fisher, director (Caldwell, Idaho: Caxton, 1939), pp. 92–93.

87. Mary Alicia Owen, *Voodoo Tales as Told among the Negroes of the Southwest* (New York and London: G. P. Putnam's Sons, 1893), pp. 246–253.

88. Daniel G. Brinton, "Reminiscences of Pennsylvania Folk-Lore," *Journal of American Folklore* 5 (1892):181.

89. Clifton Johnson, *What They Say in New England* [1896], ed. Carl Withers (New York and London: Columbia University Press, 1963), pp. 64–65.

90. Henry C. Davis, "Negro Folk-Lore in South Carolina," *Journal of American Folklore* 27 (1914):245.

91. John K. Strecker, "Reptiles of the South and Southwest in Folk-lore," Publications of the Texas Folk-Lore Society 5, ed. J. Frank Dobie (Austin, 1926), pp. 59–60.

92. Newbell N. Puckett, *Folk Beliefs of the Southern Negro* (Chapel Hill: University of North Carolina Press, 1926), pp. 42–43.

93. Portia Smiley, "Folk-Lore from Virginia, South Carolina, Georgia, Alabama, and Florida," *Journal of American Folklore* 32 (1919):381.

94. John B. Sale, *A Tree Named John* (Chapel Hill: University of North Carolina Press, 1929), p. 56.

95. Kearney, pp. 36–41.

96. Gibbons Poteet, "Jointsnake and Hoop Snake," in *Man, Bird, and Beast,* ed. J. Frank Dobie, Publications of the Texas Folk-Lore Society 8 (Austin, 1930), pp. 124–128.

97. Lowell Thomas, *Tall Stories* (New York and London: Funk and Wagnalls, 1931), pp. 165–67.

98. "North Carolina Folktales Current in the 1820's," ed. Ralph Steele Boggs, *Journal of American Folklore* 47 (1934):279.

99. Chapman J. Milling, "Is the Serpent Tale an Indian Survival?", *Southern Folklore Quarterly* 1 (1937):46–47, 53–54.

100. *Hoosier Folklore Bulletin* No. 1 (June 1942):18; No. 2 (August 1942):52, 67; No. 3 (December 1942):95.

101. Ruth Ann Musick, "Iowa Student Tales," *Hoosier Folklore* 5 (1946):108; Dorothy J. Baylor, "Folklore from Socorro, New Mexico," ibid. 6 (1947):99; Ruth Ann Musick, "West Virginia Folklore," ibid. 7 (1948):1–2.

102. *Hoosier Folklore Bulletin* No. 2 (August 1942):67.

103. Musick, "West Virginia Folklore," pp. 1–2.

104. Wm. Marion Miller, "Another Hoopsnake Story," *Journal of American Folklore* 64 (1951):423.

105. Randolph, p. 132.

106. Ibid., pp. 133–136.

107. Brown, p. 7.

108. Tryon, p. 27.

109. Schwartz, pp. 52–55.

110. Quoted in Dorson, *Jonathan Draws the Long Bow,* p. 26.

111. Reprinted in Dorson, *Jonathan Draws the Long Bow,* p. 133, from Fred A. Wilson, *Some Annals of Nahant, Mass.* (Boston, 1928), p. 161.

112. Samuel Adams Drake, *A Book of New England Legends and Folk Lore* (Boston: Roberts Brothers, 1884), pp. 156–159.

113. Dorson, *Jonathan Draws the Long Bow,* pp. 133–137.

114. Skinner, *Myths and Legends of Our Own Land,* II, 297–305; Skinner, *American Myths and Legends,* II, 277–284.

115. Charles E. Brown, *Sea Serpents* (Madison: Wisconsin Folklore Society, 1942).

116. Richard M. Dorson, *Bloodstoppers and Bearwalkers* (Cambridge: Harvard University Press, 1952), pp. 247–248.

117. Austin Fife, "The Bear Lake Monsters," *Utah Humanities Review* 2 (April 1948):99–106.

118. Ibid., p. 103.

119. Ibid., p. 104.

120. Harry S. Douglas, "The Legend of the Serpent," *New York Folklore Quarterly* 12 (1956):37–42.

121. William Harris, "The White River Monster of Jackson County, Arkansas: A Historical Summary of Oral and Popular Growth and Change in a Legend," *Mid-South Folklore* 5 (Spring 1977):3–23.

122. Ibid., p. 4.

123. Ibid.

124. Ibid., pp. 9–10.

125. ibid., p. 19.

126. Of the three illustrated bestiaries, only Schwartz includes the sea serpent.

127. John Napier, *Bigfoot, The Yeti and Sasquatch in Myth and Reality* (London: Jonathan Cape, 1972).

128. Ibid., ch. 4, "Tales from the Minnesota Woods," pp. 98–114.

129. Ibid., facing page 113.

130. Ibid., p. 95.

131. Ibid., p. 96.

132. Ibid., pp. 85–86.

133. Elwood D. Baumann, *Bigfoot, America's Abominable Snowman* (New York and London: Franklin Watts, 1975), pp. 41–45.

134. Ibid., p. 83.

135. Ibid., p. 40.

136. Napier, p. 22.

Part II. Munchausens

1. The details of this publication are given in William Rose's Introduction to *The Travels of Baron Munchausen* (London: George Routledge and Sons [1923]).

2. For Bill Greenfield's tales, see Harold W. Thompson, *Body, Boots and Britches* (Philadelphia: Lippincott, 1939), pp. 216–221; and Eugenia L. Millard, "'Big Shot' Bill Greenfield," *New York Folklore Quarterly* 12 (1956):216–221.

3. William H. Jansen, *Abraham "Oregon" Smith: Pioneer, Folk Hero and Tale Teller* (New York: Arno Press, 1977), pp. 173–183. Hereafter referred to as Jansen.

4. Stephen D. Beckham ed., *Tall Tales from Rogue River: The Yarns of Hathaway Jones* (Bloomington: Indiana University Press, 1974), pp. 17–24.

5. Bernard DeVoto, *Mark Twain's America* (Boston: Little, Brown, 1932), pp. 142–143.

6. J. Cecil Alter, *James Bridger: Trapper, Frontiersman, Scout and Guide* [1925] (Columbus, Ohio: Long's College Book Co., 1951), p. 228, quoting J. W. Gunnison.

7. J. Lee Humfreville, *Twenty Years Among Our Hostile Indians*, 2d ed. (New York: Hunter & Co., 1913), p. 462.

8. Alter, p. 518; cf. p. 380, note 26.

9. Ibid. pp. 387, 588.

10. Humfreville, p. 469.

11. Henry Inman, *The Old Santa Fe Trail* (New York: Macmillan, 1899), pp. 328–329.

12. Alter, pp. 228–229, quoting J. W. Gunnison, *History of the Mormons* (Philadelphia, 1852).

13. Humfreville, pp. 467–468.

14. Inman, pp. 331–332.

15. Inman pp. 329–330; Humfreville, p. 446.

16. Inman, p. 330.

17. Humfreville, p. 466.

18. Hiram M. Chittenden, *The Yellowstone National Park*, 6th ed. (Cincinnati: The Robert Clarke Co., 1910), p. 47.

19. N. P. Langford, *The Discovery of Yellowstone Park* (n.p., 1905).

20. Ibid., pp. 112–113.

21. Chittenden, pp. 45–46, quoting Gunnison.

22. Humfreville, pp. 464–465; Dodge in Alter, p. 522; cf. Humfreville, pp. 463–464 for the aged Bridger at 76; Frank A. Root in Alter, p. 387.

23. Alter, p. 386.

24. Ibid., p. 382.

25. Humfreville, p. 465.

26. Inman, p. 330.

27. Ernest W. Baughman, *Type and Motif-Index of the Folktales of England and North America* (The Hague: Mouton, 1966), p. 539: Motif X1410: "Lie: remarkable fruits." Hereafter referred to as Baughman.

28. Ernest W. Baughman, *Southern Folklore Quarterly* 6:163 (1942), Motif X1410 (B).

29. Langford, p. vii.

30. Baughman, p. 550: Motif X1531: "Remarkable country."

31. Chittenden, pp. 50–51.

32. Alter, p. 384.

33. Alter, p. 383, quoting Nelson A. Miles, *Personal Recollections* (New York, 1896).

34. Quoted in Alter, p. 356.

35. *James Clyman, American Frontiersman*, ed. Charles L. Camp (San

Francisco: California Historical Society, 1928), p. 26; quoted and edited in Alter, p. 588.

36. George F. Ruxton, *Life in the Far West* (Edinburgh and London: William Blackwood and Sons, 1851), pp. 5–7.

37. Alter, p. 157.

38. Ibid., pp. 67, 74, 107, 135, 194, 196, 198, 558.

39. Ibid., p. 107.

40. *James Clyman, American Frontiersman*, ed. Charles L. Camp (Portland: Champoeg Press, 1960), p. 59, quoting Marvin Ross, *The West of Alfred Jacob Miller* (Norman: University of Oklahoma Press, 1951), pp. 29, 67.

41. Camp, p. 64; also Maurice S. Sullivan, *Jedidiah Smith, Trader and Trail Breaker* (New York: Press of the Pioneers, 1936), p. 221.

42. Sullivan, p. 221, note 20.

43. Peter H. Burnett, *Recollections and Opinions of an Old Pioneer* (New York: D. Appleton and Co., 1880), p. 155.

44. Camp, p. 310, note 19.

45. Quoted in Camp, p. 309, note 18.

46. Chittenden, pp. 48–49.

47. Humfreville, pp. 464–465.

48. Hiram M. Chittenden, *Yellowstone National Park*, revised by E. C. Cress and I. F. Story (Stanford: Stanford University Press, 1933), p. 42n.

49. Ibid., pp. 43–44.

50. Richard M. Dorson, *Folklore and Fakelore* (Cambridge: Harvard University Press, 1975), p. 257.

51. Chittenden, *Yellowstone* (1933 edition), p. 44.

52. Ibid., p. 44.

53. Chittenden, *Yellowstone* (1910 edition), p. 50.

54. O. C. Hulett, *Now I'll Tell One* (Chicago: The Reilly & Lee Co., [1935]), cited in Baughman, p. 552: Motif X1543.1* (b): "Remarkable hot springs." Cf. Vance Randolph, *Hot Springs and Hell in Arkansas* (Hatboro, Pennsylvania: Folklore Associates, 1965).

55. Inman, pp. 330–331.

56. Howard Stansbury, *Exploration and Survey of the Valley of the Great Salt Lake of Utah* (Philadelphia, 1855), quoted in Alter, p. 386, note 27.

57. Baughman, p. 551, from Fred H. Hart, *The Sazerac Lying Club* (San Francisco, 1878), pp. 84–85.

58. Inman, pp. 465–466.

59. Charles M. Russell, *Trails Plowed Under* (New York, 1927), reprinted in B. A. Botkin, *A Treasury of American Folklore* (New York: Crown, 1960), p. 565. Cf. Baughman, p. 65, Type 2202: *Teller is Killed in His Story* and Motif Z13.2 (b): "The Indian kills the story-teller"; Herbert N. Halpert, "Folktales and Legends from the New Jersey Pines, A Collection and a Study" (Indiana University dissertation, 1947), pp. 349–351, 621 (tale no. 123, "The Indian Killed Me").

60. W. H. Perrin, H. H. Hill, and A. A. Graham, *The History of Edgar County, Illinois* (Chicago: LeBaron, 1879), pp. 440–447.

61. Herbert Halpert and Emma Robinson, " 'Oregon' Smith, An Indiana Folk Hero," *Southern Folklore Quarterly* 6 (1942):163–168.

62. Carl Carmer, *America Sings, Stories and Songs of Our Country's Growing* (New York: Alfred A. Knopf, 1942), pp. 78–81.

63. William H. Jansen, "More on Oregon Smith," *Hoosier Folklore Bulletin* 3 (December 1944):73–74.

64. William H. Jansen, "Lying Abe: A Teller and His Reputation," *Hoosier Folklore Bulletin* 7 (December 1948):107–124.

65. *Portrait and Biographical Album of Vermilion and Edgar Counties* (Chicago: Chapman Bros., 1889), p. 987.

66. Jansen, *Abraham "Oregon" Smith,* pp. 65–66.

67. Ibid., pp. 134, 136, 138.

68. Perrin, Hill, and Graham, pp. 440–441; reprinted in Jansen, pp. 206–207.

69. C. Lauron Hooper, *A Cloverdale Skeleton* (New York: John B. Alden, 1889), p. 28; reprinted in Jansen, pp. 214–215.

70. Jansen, p. 209, told by Guy Scott.

71. Baughman, p. 581: Motif X1733.1: "Sinking in a hard surface."

72. C. Richard K. Lunt, *Jones Tracy, Tall-Tale Hero from Mount Desert Island, Northeast Folklore* 10 [1968] (Orono, Maine: The University Press, 1969), pp. 34–35.

73. Stith Thompson, *Motif-Index of Folk-Literature,* vol. 3 (Bloomington: Indiana University Press, 1956), F 631.

74. Halpert and Robinson, pp. 164–165; collected by Emma Lou Robinson.

75. Ibid., p. 166.

76. Jansen, pp. 229–230, told by Mrs. Lilian Spencer Reed.

77. Baughman, p. 536: Motif X1402.1: "Lie, the fast-growing vine."

78. Ibid., p. 572: Motif X1651.1: "Man, shingling building during thick fog, shingles several feet of fog when he gets beyond the roof line"; cf. Roger Welsch, *Shingling the Fog and Other Plains Lies* (Chicago: Swallow Press, 1972). For Jansen's note and Smith's separate text, see Jansen, pp. 226–227.

79. Jansen, pp. 231, 233.

80. Richard M. Dorson, *Jonathan Draws the Long Bow* (Cambridge: Harvard University Press, 1946), pp. 255–256.

81. Jansen, pp. 304–305, told by W. Monroe Smith.

82. Richard M. Dorson, *Buying the Wind* (Chicago: University of Chicago Press, 1964), pp. 49–51.

83. Richard M. Dorson, *Bloodstoppers and Bearwalkers* (Cambridge: Harvard University Press, 1952), pp. 192–193.

84. Richard M. Dorson, *American Negro Folktales* (Greenwich: Fawcett, 1967), pp. 132–135.

85. Richard M. Dorson, *Folk Legends of Japan* (Rutland, Vermont, and Tokyo, 1962), pp. 174–176.

86. Jansen, p. 307. Earlier references are to "A Plow for a Pointer (Scaring the Pungnacious One)," p. 218, and "Lifting the Barrel," pp. 218–219.

87. Ibid., p. 214, quoting J. W. Ellsberry of Chrisman.

88. Jansen, pp. 238–239, told by Guy Scott.

89. Antti Aarne, Type 660 ("The Three Doctors") in *The Types of the Folktale: A Classification and Bibliography* [*Folklore Fellows Communications* no. 184], trans. Stith Thompson (Helsinki: Auomalainen Tiediakatemia, 1961), p. 231.

90. Jansen, p. 246, told by Sid Raney, Ed Scott, and Joe Vice, in collaboration.

91. Jansen, p. 328, quoting Otis Matheny.

92. Ibid., p. 331, quoting Guy Scott.

93. Ibid., p. 176.

94. Herbert Halpert, "John Darling, a New York Munchausen," *Journal of American Folklore* 57 (1944):98.

95. William Lieb in the *Sullivan County Record,* quoted in Harold W. Thompson, *Body, Boots and Britches* (Philadelphia: Lippincott, 1940), p. 135.

96. Moritz Jagendorf, "Catskill Darling: Facts about a Folk Hero," *New York Folklore Quarterly* I (1945):78.

97. Halpert, p. 99.

98. Moritz Jagendorf, *The Marvelous Adventures of Johnny Caesar Cicero Darling* (New York: Vanguard Press, 1949).

99. Halpert, p. 105, no. 18a, told by Frank Edwards.

100. Baughman, p. 473: Motif X1202, "Lie: animals inherit acquired characteristics or conditions."

101. Halpert, pp. 101–102, no. 7, told by Shock Wormuth.

102. Ibid., p. 101, no. 6, told by Fant Wormuth.

103. Ibid., p. 98, quoting George Swartwout.

104. Mody C. Boatright, *Gib Morgan, Minstrel of the Oil Fields* (n.p.: Texas Folk-Lore Society, 1945), pp. 5, 19.

105. Frank Shay, *Here's Audacity!* (New York: Macaulay, 1930), p. 63.

106. Boatright, p. 33, quoting W. G. Long.

107. Ibid., p. 47.

108. Ibid., pp. 41–42. Boatright does not include this tale among his 51 texts.

109. Baughman, p. 481: Motif X1215.11 (b); p. 479: X1215.7 (a); p. 490: X1235 (e); p. 499: X1241.1.

110. Boatright, p. 89.

111. Ibid., p. 68.

112. Ibid., pp. 75–79.

113. Ibid., pp. 64, 102.

114. C. T. Stranahan, *Pioneer Stories* (Lewiston, Idaho: Idaho Writers' League, 1947).

115. Robert G. Bailey, *River of No Return* (Lewiston, Idaho: R. G. Bailey Printing Co., 1947), p. 585.

116. Baughman, p. 581: Motif X1731.2, "Man falls from height, goes into solid rock up to knees (also in Münchhausen and in *Idaho Lore,* prepared by the Federal Writers' Project of the Works Project Administration, Vardis Fisher, director [Caldwell, Idaho, 1939], p. 116); pp. 435–436: Motifs X1003-X1004, "Lie: remarkable roper" and "Lie: remarkable rider"; p. 583: Motif X1741.2, "Person or animal jumps back to starting place from midair" (Type 1889J). There is no motif for the dog caught in the crooked trail.

117. Jan Harold Brunvand, "Len Henry: North Idaho Münchausen," *Northwest Folklore* I (1965): 11–19.

118. Ibid., p. 14.

119. Ibid., p. 17, told by Barney McGovern.

120. Lunt, *Jones Tracy.*

121. Ibid., p. 17.

122. Ibid., pp. 18–19.

123. Ibid., pp. 33–34.

124. Ibid., p. 33.
125. Halpert, p. 103, told by Shock Wormuth.
126. Type 1890 in the Aarne-Thompson and Baughman indexes.
127. Lunt, p. 30, told by Chauncy Somes.
128. Ibid., p. 31, told by Clark Manring.
129. Ibid., p. 32, told by Clark Manring.
130. Ibid., pp. 23–25; for "Blueberries," see pp. 29–30.
131. Halpert, pp. 101, 102.
132. Lunt, pp. 55–56.
133. Ibid., pp. 39–40, told by Tracy's grandson, Philip Carroll.
134. Ibid., p. 27, told by Ralph Tracy, son of Jones Tracy.
135. Warren S. Walker, with the assistance of Richard Logan and Gordon MacLeod, "Dan'l Stamps: Tall Tale Hero of the River Country," *Midwest Folklore* 4 (Fall 1954):153–160.
136. Ibid., p. 153.
137. Ibid., p. 157.
138. Ibid., pp. 155–156.
139. Baughman, p. 508: Motif X1286, "Lies about mosquitoes."
140. Ibid., p. 510: Motif X1286. 1.4.1*.
141. Walker, pp. 158–159.
142. Baughman, p. 563: Motif X1622, 1.1*(a).
143. Nancy Wilson Ross, *Farthest Reach* (New York: Alfred A. Knopf, 1941), p. 300.
144. See the bibliography in Beckham, pp. 177–178. The article in the *Saturday Evening Post* was written by Jean Muir, "The Hermits Who Hate Hollywood" (Feb. 9, 1946), pp. 26–27, 71ff.
145. Beckham, pp. 6–7, quoting Claude Riddle.
146. Ross, p. 298.
147. Beckham, pp. 144–145, from Claude Riddle, "In the Hills with Hathaway," *In the Happy Hills* (Roseburg, Oregon: M-M Printers, 1954).
148. Ross, p. 300.
149. Beckham, p. 142.
150. Ibid., p. 142.
151. Ibid., pp. 87–88, from Kathryn McPherson, "Hathaway Jones, Rogue's Paul Bunyan," *Oregon's South Coast* (Coos Bay, Oregon: World Publishing Co., 1960).
152. Beckham, pp. 95–98.
153. Ibid., pp. 105–106, told by Glen Woolridge to Jean Muir in "The Hermits Who Hate Hollywood."
154. Beckham, pp. 114–116.
155. Ibid., p. 75.
156. Ibid., pp. 75–78.
157. Ibid., pp. 111–112.
158. Ibid., pp. 117–119.
159. Ibid., p. 128, from McPherson; cf. Baughman, p. 599: Motif X1818.1* (e), "Veins of gold so rich that on warm days the gold oozes out of crevices in the cliffs."
160. Beckham, p. 95.
161. Ibid., p. 134, from Linda Barker, "Hathaway Jones," MS., Randall V. Mills Folklore Archive, University of Oregon, Eugene.
162. Baughman, p. 590: Motif X1767.2* (2), "Draft draws wood out of stove, up chimney."
163. Beckham, p. 139, from McPherson.